TExES

Physical Education EC-12 Practice Questions

Mometrix
TEST PREPARATION

DEAR FUTURE EXAM SUCCESS STORY

First of all, **THANK YOU** for purchasing Mometrix study materials!

Second, congratulations! You are one of the few determined test-takers who are committed to doing whatever it takes to excel on your exam. **You have come to the right place.** We developed these practice tests with one goal in mind: to deliver you the best possible approximation of the questions you will see on test day.

Standardized testing is one of the biggest obstacles on your road to success, which only increases the importance of doing well in the high-pressure, high-stakes environment of test day. Your results on this test could have a significant impact on your future, and these practice tests will give you the repetitions you need to build your familiarity and confidence with the test content and format to help you achieve your full potential on test day.

Your success is our success

We would love to hear from you! If you would like to share the story of your exam success or if you have any questions or comments in regard to our products, please contact us at **800-673-8175** or **support@mometrix.com**.

Thanks again for your business and we wish you continued success!

Sincerely,
The Mometrix Test Preparation Team

Printed in the United States of America

TABLE OF CONTENTS

Practice Test #1

Multiple Choice Questions

1. Which component of health-related physical fitness is most dependent on the others?

a. Flexibility/mobility
b. Body composition
c. Cardiovascular endurance
d. Muscular strength

2. The target heart rate zone, which is attained through moderate-intensity activity, improves aerobic capacity, energy, and fitness, and burns fat, is which percentage of an individual's maximum heart rate?

a. 50-65 percent
b. 85-100 percent
c. 50 percent or less
d. 65-85 percent

3. Among the benefits to students of teamwork in sports, which of these is LEAST applicable?

a. Communication and cooperation
b. Socializing in less sedentary ways
c. Learning to win above everything
d. Valuing commitment, dedication

4. PE curriculum can be modified to enable participation by students with special needs in the areas of directions, rules, equipment, and environment. Which choice reflects adaptations in the area of rules?

a. Lowering the basketball hoop
b. Installing padding, hand holds
c. Removing time requirements
d. Giving a student oral prompts

5. Among the following, which is/are designed for evaluating flexibility?

a. Goniometer/inclinometer
b. Push-up or pull-up test
c. Bench or leg presses
d. Vertical jump test

6. The teacher chooses squad lines to take attendance so she can easily see if students are absent. Which of the following is a limitation to this approach?

a. squad lines are outdated
b. squad lines are teacher-centered
c. squad lines take too much time
d. squad lines can lead to behavioral problems

7. Which technique aids in the refinement and integration of locomotor skills?

a. Utilizing demonstrations
b. Incorporating movement concepts
c. Leading and following
d. Isolation of locomotor skills

8. Ms. Jones collected students' dribbling skills tests data for five years and found many students were not proficient by the end of 8th grade. Which of the following is a logical next step for Ms. Jones to take to improve student dribbling outcomes?

a. Accepting that not all students will meet outcomes
b. Introducing dribbling skills sooner
c. Evaluating her instructional skill cues
d. Providing after-school instruction

9. Regarding conflict resolution skills, the Texas Essential Knowledge and Skills (TEKS) for PE include which of the following for students in the high school grades?

a. Handling conflicts with others without confrontations
b. Recognizing and resolving conflicts during PE activities
c. Resolving conflicts through socially acceptable methods
d. Socially acceptable conflict resolution via sportsmanship

10. Among positive social behaviors that participating in PE activities can foster in students, learning to take turns in PE classes generalizes to other classes and to life. This corresponds most closely to which social asset that PE participation promotes?

a. Cooperation
b. Leadership
c. Teamwork
d. Friendship

11. The teacher has created progressive activities where students easily find success in skill acquisition before moving on to more complex skills. Which of the following concepts is developed through this practice?

a. emotional development
b. self-regulation
c. motivation competence
d. autonomous development

12. Which of the following is a technique used to evaluate muscular endurance?

a. One-repetition maximum
b. Tracking repetition count over time
c. Recording weight lifted over time
d. Muscle fiber analysis

13. Which of the following health-related fitness components contributes to increased range of motion?

a. Flexibility
b. Body composition
c. Coordination
d. Balance

14. Which of the following activities can students engage in to evaluate their personal health risk factors?

a. maintaining a nutrition log
b. creating health goals
c. having a blood work analysis
d. tracking physical activity

15. One student has an unusually short stature and has a difficult time getting the shuttlecock over the net during their serve. Which of the following is an equitable solution to this issue?

a. moving the student closer to the net
b. allowing the student's partner to serve
c. providing a box for the student to stand on
d. lowering the net

16. Which safety rule is unique to golf, archery, and racquet activities?

a. Maintaining distance from striker or shooter
b. Avoiding facing the person striking or shooting the object
c. Keeping one's eyes on the object
d. Looking before releasing or striking

17. During the dance unit, students alternate between leading and following to develop which of the following social skills?

a. leadership
b. teamwork
c. loyalty
d. inclusion

18. Cross-country athletes want to maintain their fitness, but the snow, ice, and cold temperatures have restricted them from training outdoors. Which of the following activities will help the athletes maintain their current fitness levels needed for cross-country?

a. HIIT Training
b. Resistance training
c. Treadmill training
d. Plyometric training

19. A student sprains an ankle after landing from a balance beam jump. Which of the following is the first priority immediately after a student sprains an ankle?

a. Mobilizing the injury
b. Putting ice on the injury
c. Putting heat on the injury
d. Calling 911

20. The Society of Health and Physical Educators (SHAPE America) offers tools for advocates of PE. Which of the following among these tools could an advocate best use to show stakeholders and decision makers why and how school health and physical education is important and beneficial for all students?

a. *The Essential Components of Physical Education,* guidance document
b. *PE + Health = Student Success (Speak Out! for Health & PE)*, fact sheet
c. *Physical Education is an Academic Subject*, SHAPE position statement
d. *Advocacy in Action* columns from SHAPE America's *Strategies* journal

21. For fifth-grade students, which of the following shows the ability to integrate locomotor, non-locomotor, and stability movements within more complex movement skills?

a. Showing mature motor patterns on obstacle courses
b. Playing simple games that require manipulative skills
c. Describing the important parts of throwing overhand
d. Understanding that practicing improves performance

22. In a public school's PE risk management and emergency procedure plans, which is typically among the provisions?

a. If any students are injured, the school nurse offers the initial first aid.
b. All physical educators carry emergency first aid kits during PE classes.
c. Not all physical educators need have current first aid and CPR certificates.
d. PE teachers may not know which students lack treatment permission.

23. Adaptation through exercise is a major principle of which of these sciences, which also applies the others?

a. Anatomy
b. Physiology
c. Kinesiology
d. Neurology

24. Which of the following is a strategy used for refinement and integration of manipulative skills?

a. mirroring
b. choice
c. leading and following
d. small-sided games

25. Kenya is having difficulty with balance and coordination skills in the gymnastic routines. Which perceptual motor ability may be underdeveloped?

a. Hearing
b. Vision
c. Touch sensitivity
d. Audiation

26. What are the minimum cardiovascular activity recommendations for students in middle school?

a. 20-minutes a day
b. 30-minutes a day
c. 45-minutes a day
d. 60-minutes a day

27. Among manipulative skills used in sports, which of these does NOT use the hands?

a. Dribbling as in basketball
b. Trapping as in soccer
c. Throwing in general
d. Catching in general

28. Which of the following movement concepts help facilitate relationships with objects in the environment?

a. forward and backward
b. over and under
c. straight and curved
d. strong and light

29. Recognizing and understanding the significance of regular physical activity to healthy lifestyles is an objective most appropriate to which grade levels in public schools?

a. Grades EC-K
b. Grades K-2
c. Grades 3-5
d. Grades 6-12

30. Students have physical education two days a week and are not meeting physical activity recommendations. Which of the following are realistic community resources that provide physical activity opportunities for all students?

a. parks and recreation
b. hiking trails
c. rock climbing
d. fitness centers

31. Which of the following PE activities demonstrates motor or movement skills that a typically developing student should be able to perform by the end of the third grade?

a. Using a bat to hit a ball pitched by another
b. Catch, dribble, pass ball to moving partner
c. Jumping a rope while others are twirling it
d. Jumping a rope that one is twirling oneself

32. Several students are jerky in their movements during the dance performance. On which movement concept does the teacher need to focus to help students move more smoothly?

a. Force
b. Time
c. Flow
d. Levels

33. Research shows that exercise lowers the risk of high blood pressure, stroke, and heart disease. What is true about other health benefits of exercise?

a. Exercise lowers the risk of all kinds of cancers.
b. Exercise cannot change the risk of dementia.
c. Exercise lowers the risk for Type 1 diabetes.
d. Exercise lowers the risk of breaking bones.

34. Regarding the relationship of body awareness, motor skills development, perceptual skills development, and other learning in school, which statement is correct?

a. Perceptual skill development leads to body awareness and motor development.
b. The development of fine motor skills leads to development of gross motor skills.
c. Perceptual skills develop out of good motor skills, which rely on body awareness.
d. Perceptual skills, but not motor skills, help in reading, writing, and other learning.

35. According to experienced PE teachers, which of the following is true about classroom management in PE classes for the elementary grades?

a. Making eye contact is more important than learning student names for rapport.
b. Post gym rules and consequences clearly and deliver consequences consistently.
c. Stay on the move constantly throughout class; do not have your back to the wall.
d. Making positive comments reinforces good behavior but does not encourage it.

36. Which of the following statements is most accurate about the role of self-assessment in developing physical fitness and lifelong participation in physical activity?

a. Self-assessment should not be required since students lack the training.
b. Self-assessment encourages reflection, which interferes with execution.
c. Self-assessment enables students to determine their current skill levels.
d. Self-assessment causes loss of control over the developmental process.

37. Which of the following methods best improves high complex skill combinations?

a. part practice
b. whole practice
c. whole-part-whole practice
d. small-sided games practice

38. Researchers tested a three-year intervention, Physical Activity Across the Curriculum (PAAC), with 4,905 children in elementary schools using a randomized, controlled trial. Which choice do you think most likely describes one of their findings?

a. Students enjoyed physically active lessons more than teachers did.
b. More physical activity in schools competed with instructional time.
c. Bandura's self-efficacy is significant for setting and achieving goals.
d. PA integration is expensive, and requires replacing the curriculum.

39. Stephanie started a workout routine for her New Year's resolution. Her body was extremely sore and she could barely walk the next day. Which of the following principles of fitness did Stephanie ignore?

a. Delayed onset muscle syndrome
b. Overload
c. Progression
d. Specificity

40. Which of the following are the movement pathways used to teach locomotor movements?

a. straight, curved, zigzag
b. right, left, forward, diagonal
c. straight, forward, backward
d. zigzag, forward, backward

41. A student is thinking about hiring a personal trainer at the local gym. Which of the following should the student consider before hiring a personal trainer?

a. The gym's reputation
b. Customer reviews
c. Insurance
d. Certification

42. When does physical education instruction necessarily require giving feedback to students?

a. When a skill requires specific correction
b. When a skill gets environmental feedback
c. When a student has experience with a skill
d. When a teacher can comprehensively demonstrate a skill

43. Among elements of the FITT principle, which one is determined by two of the others?

a. How long each workout session should last
b. How to ensure overload without overwork
c. How often to work out for stress plus rest
d. How training is cardio, resistance, or both

44. Among PE activities applying the concept of effort qualities, which type primarily applies the mechanical principle of time?

a. Having students use their bodies to create impetus moving them through space
b. Having students apply specified movement patterns as fast and slow as they can
c. Having students utilize paddles to propel balls to make them bounce off of walls
d. Having students practice jumping over different objects having different heights

45. Which of the following helps establish student responsibility and self-control?

a. Playing a team sport
b. The course guide or syllabus
c. Parental feedback
d. Expectations and assessment

46. Which of the following combined motor skills is on the upper end of the skill progression continuum?

a. Skipping baseline to baseline
b. Running 400 meters
c. Dribbling a soccer ball
d. Jumping over an obstacle

47. Which of the following best describes the differences between motor learning and motor performance?

a. Motor performance can be observed.
b. Motor learning can be observed.
c. Motor learning is the demonstration of motor skills.
d. Motor performance is permanent.

48. Of the following choices, which one most describes a stage of motor learning associated with the age period of adolescence?

a. Purposeful movements develop beyond simple reflexes.
b. Motor patterns of increasing complexity are developing.
c. Motor patterns gain increasing automaticity and fluidity.
d. Ability, motivation, and practice influence development.

49. Which of the following body composition measures estimates body fat composition using a person's height and weight?

a. Skinfold calipers
b. Hydrostatic weighing
c. Waist circumference
d. Body mass index

50. Ari's tennis ball lands beyond the baseline (out of bounds or long) during her tennis forehand. What strategy will help Ari keep the ball in-bound?

a. Adding topspin
b. Reducing the power at the point of contact
c. Increasing the speed of the racket
d. Bringing the striking arm closer to the body

51. Which of the following is a physiological benefit of exercise that helps manage stress responses?

a. it improves mood
b. it enhances positive thoughts
c. it lowers the release of cortisol
d. it increases confidence

52. Which of the following statements best describes Bandura's social learning theory?

a. Learning through touch
b. Learning through reading
c. Learning through mental imagery
d. Learning through observation

53. A student is having difficulty staying afloat during the swimming unit. Which of the following identifies a potential problem and a solution to the student's issue?

a. The student has increased drag and needs to empty the air in their lungs
b. The student has high buoyancy and needs to empty the air in their lungs
c. The student lacks drag and needs to fill up their lungs with air
d. The student lacks buoyancy and needs to fill up their lungs with air

54. Which type of muscle is responsible for voluntary muscular contraction that occurs during physical activity?

a. Smooth
b. Skeletal
c. Cardiac
d. Sliding filament

55. Max fell forward when performing an isometric squat. Which of the following biomechanical factors contributed to this forward motion?

a. the heels are flat
b. the chest is too low
c. the feet are too wide
d. the hips are not far back enough

56. Which of the following activities fosters motivation to engage in lifelong physical activity?

a. Grades
b. Fitness testing
c. Self-assessment
d. Ability tracking

57. Typical safety guidelines for ascending climbing ropes in portable or permanent installations on school or commercial sites are best reflected by which choice?

a. A working phone is only needed for installations outside of the school.
b. An accessible first aid kit is unnecessary at installations within schools.
c. All climbing ropes are compatible with all activities, plus belay devices.
d. Equipment must meet standards and be made for the planned activity.

58. Using a lever gives a mechanical advantage (MA), expressed as the ratio of the power arm's length to the weight arm's length. In other words, MA = a ratio of motive force to resistive force. What is true about this principle?

a. If the quotient is <1, motive force is < resistive force.
b. If the quotient is >1, resistive force is > motive force.
c. If the quotient is =1, there is the greatest advantage.
d. If the quotient is >1, resistive force is < motive force.

59. When learning new PE skills, students need more ______ feedback; when they have developed more competence and confidence in certain PE skills and can analyze their own performance, they can make better use of ______ feedback.

a. Extrinsic; intrinsic
b. Intrinsic; extrinsic
c. Positive; negative
d. Constructive; corrective

60. During the spatial awareness unit, Jason could not identify the small movements essential in large gross motor activities. Which of the following perceptual-motor skills is difficult for Jason?

a. Fine motor discrimination
b. Auditory discrimination
c. Visual discrimination
d. Kinesthetic discrimination

61. Which of the following is an objective method for students to self-assess their physical activity levels over time?

a. using calorie counters
b. writing journal entries
c. using heart rate monitors
d. writing reflections

62. Which of the following descriptions is most applicable to learning standards for PE students in grades 9-12?

a. Students show the ability to explore fundamental locomotor and non-locomotor skills.
b. Students are capable of demonstrating the mature forms in locomotor and non-locomotor skills.
c. Students can apply the mature forms of motor skills in specialized sports, dance, and gymnastics.
d. Students use locomotor, non-locomotor, manipulative skills in sports, dance, and gymnastics activities.

63. A student trips over her shoelaces and hits her head on the volleyball standards during gameplay. Which of the following should the teacher have done to reduce the risk of liability?

a. tied the student's shoelaces
b. nothing as it was an accident
c. covered the standards with padding
d. posted the potential risks

64. Which of the following are techniques used to ensure equal opportunities for students to participate, learn, and succeed in physical education class?

a. Inviting administrators to observe classes
b. Inviting parents to observe classes
c. Appointing student captains
d. Modifying activities

65. In a risk management plan for a school PE program, which division or section would include emergency procedures and accident reports in cases of student injury?

a. Conduct of activities and services
b. Conditions from the environment
c. Management of student behavior
d. Practices of supervision in general

66. Which of the following laws or guidelines protects students' medical and personal information?

a. HIPAA
b. IDEA
c. ADHD
d. FERPA

67. Which kinds of physical education activities are both appropriate for boys and girls to participate in together and are less dependent on team assignment by student skill levels?

a. Activities that involve participant body contact
b. Activities that require more upper-body strength
c. Activities that require agility and lower-body strength
d. Activities of all these types

68. To adapt a PE class in basketball for students with disabilities, which adaptation applies most to students using wheelchairs?

a. Play using a "beeper ball" that produces beeping sounds
b. Positioning a radio or other audio device under the basket
c. Removing any obstacles, especially small, from the court
d. Letting students hold the ball in their laps while traveling

69. Body mass index (BMI) calculates an individual's proportion of body fat to height and weight. Which of the following BMI ranges corresponds to a normal body composition?

a. 18.5 or less
b. 25.0 to 29.9
c. 18.5 to 24.9
d. 30 or more

70. Current recommendations for children and adults are for how much physical activity at a moderate intensity per day?

a. 20 minutes
b. 30 minutes
c. 45 minutes
d. 15 minutes

71. Which of the following correctly reflects research findings about the relationship of exercise to stress?

a. Aerobic exercise can elevate but not stabilize mood.
b. Aerobic exercise can enhance sleep and self-esteem.
c. Aerobic exercise can reduce anxiety if performed more than 10 minutes.
d. Aerobic exercise can aid cognition yet cause fatigue.

72. How can a PE teacher best use technology like tablet and smartphone apps that record video, including uploading to computers for playback, for the specific purpose of analyzing student performance and progress?

a. Show them video of professional athletes performing skills they are learning.
b. Show them videos of their activity to identify strengths, development needs.
c. Show them video of classmate activity to identify what things they do wrong.
d. Show them video of the class at the end of a lesson as instructional feedback.

73. The teacher focuses on building self-efficacy to improve performance during gameplay. Which of the following strategies has shown to develop self-efficacy?

a. Vicarious learning
b. Team cohesion
c. Isolation learning
d. Respecting the player

74. Which of the following techniques to measure aerobic duration is appropriate for large class sizes?

a. Activity trackers
b. Pedometers
c. Stopwatches
d. Aerobic equipment monitors

75. A third grader broke down and had a temper tantrum after having a series of unsuccessful forward rolls. Which of the following factors might be impeding the student's physical development?

a. emotional knowledge
b. emotional self-regulation
c. self-efficacy
d. self-esteem

76. Which of the following is a benefit of elective physical education programs?

a. Ensures enough equipment for all students
b. Caters to the teacher's strengths
c. Students decide their program
d. Helps with non-PE course schedules

77. Which of the following is an appropriate method used to assess heart rate (HR) intensity during exercise?

a. Continuous aerobic activity
b. Talk test
c. Percentage of maximum heart rate
d. Recovery heart rate

78. Spectators booed a player for missing a free throw. Which of the following best describes the behavior of the spectators?

a. Unsportsmanlike behavior
b. Poor etiquette
c. Rule violation
d. Spectator violation

79. A spectator passes out during the football game and the CPR certified PE teacher is called to help. Which of the following steps should the PE teacher do first?

a. call 911
b. check the scene
c. check for breathing
d. start CPR

80. The federal government defines basic elements of furthering student development through physical activity (PA) that PE programs and teachers promote. How are these elements structured to accomplish major PE goals?

a. Attaining participant developmental health outcomes enables creating optimum contexts for PA, which enables providing universal PA opportunities and access.
b. Creating optimum contexts for PA enables providing universal PA opportunities and access, which enables attaining participant developmental health outcomes.
c. Providing universal PA opportunities and access enables creating optimum contexts for PA, which enables attaining participant developmental health outcomes.
d. Attaining participant developmental health outcomes enables providing universal PA opportunities and access, which enables creating optimum contexts for PA.

81. Which of the following fitness tracking devices can inform the teacher of the intensity of students' movements?

a. Heart rate monitor
b. Accelerometer
c. Pedometer
d. Step counter

82. Which of the following strategies is recommended when selecting weight training activities for beginning students?

a. Utilizing dumbbells
b. Utilizing bodyweight
c. Utilizing a one-repetition max strength test
d. Alternating light and heavy weight

83. Which movement concept is the focus of locomotor and non-locomotor partner activities?

a. Relationships
b. High and low levels
c. Lead-up activities for team sports
d. Leading and following

84. Which of the following statements best describes the impact of verbal feedback compared to nonverbal feedback?

a. Verbal feedback is more effective than nonverbal feedback
b. Verbal feedback is less effective than nonverbal feedback
c. Verbal and nonverbal feedback aid in student learning
d. Nonverbal feedback is the gold standard

85. Which of the following strategies helps accommodate multiple abilities in physical education classes?

a. Teaching to the outcome
b. Providing extensions
c. Employing standards-based instruction
d. Incorporating differentiation

86. The teacher moved the targets closer to students unable to hit the target with an overhand throw, but students were still unable to reach the target after this change. Which of the following is an appropriate modification to try next?

a. having students throw to each other
b. keeping the targets in place until students can hit them
c. reviewing the skill cues with the students
d. varying the sizes of the balls thrown

87. Which of the following agencies sets the national K-12 physical education standards?

a. CAEP
b. GOPHER
c. NASPE
d. SHAPE

88. The cross-country coach had a spaghetti dinner for the team the night before a competition. Which of the following is the rationale for this activity?

a. To recruit energy fast
b. To run on an empty stomach
c. To ensure an equitable, healthy meal
d. To aid in better sleep

89. Throughout the school year, the teacher randomly teaches dances submitted by students at the beginning of the school year rather than focus solely on the recommended dances, e.g., square dance, in the curriculum. Which of the following concepts is the teacher promoting?

a. self-efficacy
b. diversity
c. choice
d. autonomy

90. Which of the following practice styles has been shown to be the most effective in improving student performance in PE and sport settings?

a. Random practice
b. Variable practice
c. Blocked practice
d. Mental practice

Constructed Response

91. Cynthia plans to introduce yoga to her physical education classes this week. She hopes to incorporate yoga poses such as downward dog and tree pose. Through these lessons, students will work on their ability to demonstrate actions such as twisting and stretching.

Based on the plans above and your knowledge of these types of movements:

- Explain the differences between locomotor and non-locomotor movement.
- Identify if Cynthia's lesson will focus on locomotor or non-locomotor movement.
- Describe a way that Cynthia could also incorporate an alternative type of movement into her lessons.

Answer Key and Explanations for Test #1

Multiple Choice Questions

1. B: Body composition is the individual body's ratio of lean body mass to body fat. It depends most on the other four components, i.e., flexibility (a), cardiovascular endurance (c), muscular strength (d), and muscular endurance, because improving these will naturally improve the body composition after consistent fitness conditioning over time.

2. D: Maximum heart rate is calculated by subtracting age from 220; e.g., for a 14-year-old student, 220-14 = 206 beats per minute (bpm). The target heart rate zone is 65-85 percent of maximum; 50-65 percent (a) is recommended for people unaccustomed to exercising or very out of shape; 85-100 percent (b) is a high-intensity zone recommended for athletes and other highly fit individuals; and 50 percent or less (c) is the zone for warming up and cooling down before and after exercise.

3. C: Students benefit from teamwork in sports by learning important social skills for life, like communicating and cooperating with others (A); socializing actively instead of playing video games, watching TV, etc. (B); and learning the value of commitment, dedication (D), and hard work through competing together as a group. However, it is also important for students to realize that in sports, winning should not always be the only goal above everything else (C).

4. C: Eliminating requirements to complete some activities within certain time limits reflects a curricular adaptation for special-needs students in the area of rules. Lowering a basketball hoop (a) reflects a modification in the area of equipment. Installing padding and hand holds (b), as well as making other adaptive equipment accessible, are modifications in the area of environment. Giving oral prompts (d) reflects modification in the area of directions.

5. A: Goniometers measure angles of body joints; inclinometers measure arcs of motion during complex movements, both for assessing flexibility or range of motion. In lieu of these, the sitting reach test can be used. Push-up and pull-up tests (b) are designed for evaluating muscular endurance. Bench presses and leg presses (c) are designed for assessing muscle strength. The vertical jump test (d) is for evaluating leg power.

6. D: Students can get bored sitting in squad lines which increases off-task behaviors or behavioral problems. An active squad line approach and frequently changing squad lines may keep students engaged and lessen boredom and off-task behaviors. Locating absent students is generally a faster approach than taking attendance for all present students. Squad lines are considered vintage or an outdated approach but can be effective for extremely large class sizes and combined with learning outcomes, e.g., active warm-up. Squad-lines may or may not be teacher-centered, which depends on how the squads are created and whether squad line leaders are used. Using squad leaders is a recommendation to speed up taking attendance, provide student-leadership, and reduce boredom.

7. B: The movement concepts of spatial awareness, relationships, and effort help refine and integrate skills, as combining these elements increases the locomotor movements' challenge, thus fostering mature movement patterns needed for manipulative activities. Demonstrations, as well as leading and following, aid in the refinement of the basic locomotor movements but will not independently help the student achieve skill integration and refine higher-level skills without incorporating the movement concepts.

8. C: Ms. Jones should evaluate her instructional skill cues and other teaching practices to determine if they meet the intended outcome or if they need to change to ensure that students are proficient by the end of 8th grade. Dribbling is a skill taught in elementary(B), so students should build on those skills in grades 6, 7, and 8. After-school instruction may be beneficial (D), but it would not be the next logical step as a change in instruction needs to occur prior to this because students could potentially continue to practice poor instructional cues. While not all students will meet the outcomes, the goal is to continue to work towards these outcomes (A).

9. B: Under Social Development, PE TEKS include handling conflicts without confrontation (A) for grade 6; recognizing and resolving conflicts during activities (B) for high school students, ONLY in the Foundations of Personal Fitness course; resolving conflicts in socially acceptable ways like talking and requesting teacher assistance (C) for grade 1; and socially acceptable conflict resolution using sportsmanship skills (D) for grade 5. Grades 2, 3, and 4 PE TEKS include cooperation, respect, appropriate behavior, and sportsmanship; and etiquette and responsible behavior for other high school courses, not conflict resolution specifically.

10. A: The President's Council on Physical Fitness and Sport reports social assets promoted by PE participation, including skills for leading others (b), working together toward a common goal (c), developing closer, higher-quality friendships (d), and cooperating with others (a), which most closely corresponds to learning to take turns in PE classes, hence in other classes and in life.

11. C: Motivation competence is developed when students experience success in easier tasks that builds confidence to try more difficult tasks. Self-regulation is awareness of how one learns and acceptance of the responsibility for the learning. Emotional development is the ability to manage feelings and emotions to focus on learning. Autonomous development is when learners perform tasks easily or automatically, as they have mastered the skill and no longer have to think about it.

12. B: Tracking repetition count over time is a technique used to evaluate muscular endurance. Athletes may fatigue after 6 to 10 reps at the beginning of a workout routine and do several sets of 20 reps at the same weight a few weeks later, which indicates that they have improved their muscular endurance and need to increase either the amount of weight lifted or the number of reps. Although recording weight lifted over time will likely be included, doing so is a method to evaluate muscular strength not muscular endurance. A one-repetition maximum assessment is also a technique used to measure muscular strength, but it is not recommended in physical education programs. A muscle fiber biopsy is the only accurate fiber analysis method, but there are fitness tests, such as vertical jump analysis, that can estimate fiber type.

13. A: Flexibility is the range of motion at the joints and is achieved by stretching the muscles and weight training. Body composition is the ratio between lean muscle and fat and is often expressed as a percentage of body fat. A normal body composition reduces the risk of debilitating metabolic conditions. Coordination is the ability to move multiple limbs and/or manipulate objects while maintaining balance. Balance is the ability to maintain posture and control the body while in motion or while stationary.

14. A: To help students evaluate personal health risk factors, they can maintain a nutrition log and evaluate and analyze the quantity (calories) and quality (fats, carbs, proteins) of their food intake to determine the foods that are healthy and unhealthy. There are several nutrition apps available for easier analysis. Goals would be created after an evaluation occurs. Blood work is another tool that identifies health risks, but this option is not feasible in a school setting and is only recommended once before puberty and once after puberty before routine blood work occurs. Tracking physical inactivity or sedentary behaviors is better than tracking physical activity as too much sedentary behavior, such as sitting for long periods, is a health risk factor even for those who engage in daily physical activity.

15. A: An equitable instructional practice is to allow the student to move closer to the net to meet diverse learners' needs. Lowering the net would be inequitable to the other three students capable of serving in the normal position. Allowing the partner to serve prevents the shorter student from developing and participating, which is an inequitable practice. Badminton is a fast sport that requires quick movements and reaction time, so a box would be unsafe as it would be on the court preventing movement and increasing the risk of injury.

16. A: Students should be taught to maintain distance from the striker or shooter to avoid getting hit with the striking object such as a golf club, arrow, or ball. While students should avoid facing a person shooting in archery, in racquet sports like tennis and badminton, students face their opponents on opposite sides of the net. Keeping eyes on the ball or the target is an important skill cue; however, it is not a safety rule when striking or shooting. There is no time to look around before striking in racquet activities, in contrast to golf and archery, where the golfer or shooter controls these actions.

17. A: Students are developing leadership skills by having the opportunity to lead a dance. They are also engaged in taking turns. Although the goal is to perform a dance together, the leader makes all of the decisions and is not reliant on the follower for a successful outcome. Loyalty is the devotion to a person or organization. Inclusion is the practice of including everyone.

18. C: Treadmill training allows cross-country athletes to run, which is specific to the activity. Athletes can achieve the same distances they would during cross-country runs. Most treadmills also have cross-country programs included. HIIT and resistance training will help cross-country athletes train and maintain health-related fitness, but unlike cross-country, the movements are non-specific and non-continuous. Plyometric training is used to develop power and is better suited for sports and activities that require explosive power, such as running cuts in basketball, sprinting, or jumping.

19. B: First aid procedures include RICE (rest, ice, compression, and elevation) to reduce inflammation. Immobilization restricts movement and further damage. Moving or mobilization (A) may cause more damage. Heat (C) is used for long-term musculoskeletal injuries but for new injuries or when in doubt, use ice. Heat can increase swelling and inflammation of new injuries. Calling 911 (D) is for life-threatening injuries. Sprains heal in time. Severe sprains and follow-up visits tend to occur with a primary care or orthopedic doctor.

20. B: Advocates can share this fact sheet with stakeholders and decision makers to show school health and physical education's importance and benefits to all students; use the guidance document (A) identifying necessary PE program elements to inform schools' structuring of PE programs; the position statement (C) to argue against cutting or reducing, and for expanding, maintaining, or funding PE because school, district, and state requirements for PE are the same as for other academic subjects; and the journal articles (D) to get practical advocacy advice and examples of advocacy challenges and successes.

21. A: Fifth-graders show ability to perform more complex movement skills integrating locomotor, non-locomotor, and stability movements by demonstrating mature motor patterns on obstacle courses and other increasingly complex settings. Playing simple games requiring manipulative skills (b) shows ability to manipulate objects using skills for sports lead-up activities and games. Describing important parts of throwing overhand (c) shows ability to describe and demonstrate elements of mature movement patterns. Understanding that practicing improves performance (d) shows ability to identify how to refine movement skills using movement concepts.

22. B: School emergency procedures typically provide that injured students are initially offered first aid by physical educators with current first aid certification, and only seen by a school nurse for follow-up as needed (A); that all physical educators carry emergency first aid kits during PE classes (B); that ALL physical educators must have current first aid and CPR certification (C); and that PE teachers and other physical educators have a list of any students who did not return emergency treatment permission forms the first week of school (D).

23. C: Anatomy (a) is the study of body structures, physiology (b) the study of body functions. Neurology (d) is the study of the nervous system, including the brain. Kinesiology (c) is the study of body movement, functions, and performance; it applies these other sciences. A major principle of kinesiology is adaptation through exercise.

24. D: Small-sided games are modified versions of games that allow for more opportunities to respond. Instead of five vs. five basketball, implementing two vs. two or three vs. three games increases student opportunity to integrate manipulative skills. Choice is a strategy used to increase student motivation. Leading and following can be used for isolation skills but do not foster integration in game-like situations. Mirroring works best with locomotor and non-locomotor movements. Demonstrations are more useful for refinement and integration of manipulative skills.

25. B: Vision is the perceptual motor ability that aids in movement detection and movement response. If Kenya is closing her eyes, that may be causing increased balance and coordination difficulty, as those sensory responses are not activated. Hearing perception is important for motor skill development but is more closely related to the body preparing to take action, for example, when hearing "go" or "start," or the sound of a thrown or caught ball.

26. D: It is recommended that middle and high school students engage in 60-minutes or more of cardiovascular activities every day. The 60-minutes can be in one session or accumulated throughout the day. Elementary students should also engage in 60-minutes a day but have shorter bouts of 15 to 20 minutes of continuous activity. Adults should engage in 30-minutes or more a day. Although these physical activity recommendations are endorsed by physical education and physical activity governing bodies, 20-minute and 45-minute sessions also positively impact health, and daily activity is encouraged across groups. Shorter sessions can be maximized with higher intensity activities.

27. B: Dribbling in basketball (A) is bouncing a ball, typically down to the floor using the hands. Throwing (C) uses one or both arms and hands to project a ball or other object away from the body into the air. Even throwing using equipment, as in jai alai, requires hands. Catching (D) stops a moving object's momentum using the hands. Trapping in soccer (B), however, uses the feet or other body parts, but NOT the hands, to control or receive the ball.

28. B: The teacher is facilitating relationships with objects by moving over and under equipment. Forward and backward reinforce spatial awareness directions. Straight and curved support spatial awareness pathways, and strong and light are effort or force movement concepts.

29. D: Recognizing and understanding the significance of regular physical activity to healthy lifestyles is an objective most appropriate for grades 6-12 in public schools. For grades EC-K (A), recognizing that physical activity has health benefits is more appropriate. For K-2 (B), recognizing the benefits of moderate to vigorous physical activity is appropriate. For grades 3-5 (C), recognizing and applying essential movement concepts and elements for their own sustained participation in physical activities is appropriate.

30. A: Most communities have parks and recreation centers that provide physical activity programming for children, adults, and families which are usually free, low cost, and/or have sliding scale fees based on income. Parks and recreation leaders have degrees and/or training in providing physical activity services. Some areas have hiking trails but these areas tend to be unsupervised and can be unsafe for children. Special equipment is needed for rock climbing and can be expensive. Some parks and recreation facilities offer indoor rock-climbing walls. Fitness centers are appropriate for high-school-aged students but some are for adults only or require a parental waiver for youth under 18 and require a fee. Many parks and recreation facilities have fitness centers for youth.

31. A: Typically developing students should be able to hit a ball pitched by another by the end of the third grade. They should be able to demonstrate sport-specific movement skill combinations, e.g., catch, dribble, and pass a basketball to a moving partner (B) by the end of the fourth grade. They should be able to jump a rope twirled by others (C) by the end of kindergarten. They should be able to jump a rope they twirl themselves (D) by the end of the second grade.

32. C: The teacher needs to focus on teaching students the concept of flow, which is the contrast between smooth and jerky movements. Force focuses on the amount of effort or intensity of a movement. Time is the rate or speed of a given activity, which can aid in teaching flow by asking students to move at a slow pace, but time is not the concept that needs clarification. The term *levels* addresses the different heights at which a movement is performed.

33. D: Research proves weight-bearing exercise strengthens bones, lowering risk for osteoporosis and associated bone fractures. Exercise lowers risk for colon cancer, breast cancer, and some others, but is not proven to lower risk for every kind of cancer (A). It lowers risk for Alzheimer's-type dementia including memory loss (B), as well as depression. It lowers risk for Type 2 diabetes, not Type 1 (Type 1 has a stronger genetic component, so even physically active children can develop it; however, carefully monitored and controlled exercise helps them manage this condition).

34. C: Body awareness is fundamental to many other skills that students need in school. Children with good awareness of their own body parts, how those parts can move, and their bodies' relationship to their surroundings develop good motor skills, which directly lead to developing good perceptual skills, not vice versa (A). Gross motor skills develop first, leading to fine motor skills development, not vice versa (B). Reading, writing, and other learning are supported by both motor and perceptual skills (D).

35. B: Experienced elementary PE teachers advise new teachers to establish rapport with students by learning all their names as soon as possible AND making eye contact (a); establish rules and consequences for breaking them, post these in the gym or classroom, review them periodically as a reminder, and always deliver consequences consistently (b) to keep order; BOTH keep moving during class AND teach with backs to the wall (c) to eliminate blind spots and keep an eye on all students; and make positive comments, both to reinforce students following rules AND encourage students who are not to do so (d).

36. C: According to PE experts, self-assessment has great power as a tool in student motor skills development, because requiring students to assess their own abilities and skills encourages them to reflect, which does NOT interfere with executing the skills (b), but does enable them to determine their current skill levels (c), as well as to take, not lose, control of the developmental process (d). Students need not be PE teachers or have specialized training to conduct self-assessment (a).

37. A: Part practice, or the breaking down of a complex skill like a volleyball spike, has shown to be the most effective method for improving high complex skill combinations. Whole practice or fully completing the skill is best for low complex skills such as running. The whole-part-whole method is ideal for tactical concepts like offense and defense used in team sports where players play the game first. During gameplay, weaknesses are identified, broken down in parts, and practiced before resuming gameplay. Small-sided games allow students to put skills into practice, but mastery of complex skills is unlikely to occur, as the game's pace is too fast; thus, the skill needs to be broken down at a slower rate.

38. C: According to goal-setting theorists, individuals high in Bandura's concept of self-efficacy (belief in one's own ability to perform a specific behavior successfully) set higher goals, are more committed to goals, and identify and apply better strategies for achieving them. The researchers (Gibson et al., 2008) found teachers and students enjoyed physically active lessons equally (A). By modifying existing content lessons to integrate PA, it did NOT compete with instructional time (B). The PAAC intervention needed no curriculum change and little school cost (D).

39. C: Stephanie ignored the progression principle, which is the gradual increase in overload when beginning a workout routine. Stephanie engaged in overload or engaged in activities greater than normal but did too much. Specificity is engaging in activities that support the goal. For example, if the goal is to run the mile faster, running fast needs to be a part of the workout or training program.

40. A: The pathways used to teach locomotor movements are straight, curved, and zigzag. Moving right, left, forward, backward and diagonal are directions the body can travel and are used to teach locomotor movements, dance, and sports skills.

41. D: The student should determine if the personal trainer holds a personal training certification, which indicates that the trainer is knowledgeable and should aid in effectiveness and safety. Gyms often cover insurance unless the personal trainer is an independent contractor. A gym's reputation may attract good trainers, but it does not guarantee the personal trainer's effectiveness. Some gyms require certification, while others do not. Customer reviews help, but customer needs and experiences vary.

42. A: While feedback is important in physical education (PE) instruction, knowing when and when not to provide feedback is equally important to effective teaching. PE teachers need to give feedback to give students specific corrections to incorrectly performed techniques, for example. However, when a task furnishes inherent environmental feedback (B),—for example, a student throws a basketball, and it goes through the hoop—additional feedback may be unnecessary. When a student already has enough experience with a skill (C), sometimes PE teachers need not give them feedback. Also, when a teacher's demonstration enables students to see easily how to perform a skill correctly (D), they may need little or no additional feedback.

43. A: FITT = Frequency, Intensity, Time, Type. How long to work out (A) = Time, which is determined by the Intensity and Type of exercise. How to ensure overload without overtraining (B), burnout, or injury = Intensity. How often to work out to ensure enough stress to make the body adapt plus allow healing through enough rest (C) = Frequency. Specific exercises to do, and whether the workout is cardio, resistance (weight), or both combined (D) = Type.

44. B: Having students apply specified movement patterns, which have been timed in advance, as fast and as slowly as they can, applies the mechanical principle of time. Choices (A), (C), and (D) are all PE activities that apply the mechanical principle of force. (Another movement effort quality applies the mechanical principle of balance.)

45. D: Expectations, assessment, and accountability help establish student responsibility and self-control. The Teaching Personal and Social Responsibility (TPSR) model employs behavioral expectations where students self-assess their behaviors and progress so they can work to improve in deficient areas. Playing a team sport without rules and expectations does not garner self-control and student-responsibility. The course guide or syllabus contains the rules and expectations, but it does not help students achieve responsibility and self-control. Parents can provide meaningful information regarding their child's learning style and ability, but some parents may enable and engage in practices that limit student responsibility and self-control. Ultimately, the teacher is responsible for creating an environment that develops student responsibility.

46. C: Dribbling a soccer ball is on the upper end of the skill progression continuum, as it combines a locomotor movement with an object (a manipulative skill) and is one of the most difficult fundamental movement skills. Skipping, running, and jumping are basic locomotor or fundamental movements.

47. A: Motor performance can be observed, but motor learning cannot. Observing motor performance over time can aid in the determination of motor learning. Motor learning is permanent, e.g., riding a bicycle; however, motor performance changes based on the environment, such as lack of rest or facing a tough defender.

48. D: In stage 1 of motor learning, babies and toddlers develop beyond simple reflexive movements (e.g., rooting, sucking, startling, Babinski, Moro, palmar, plantar) to fundamental purposeful movements like sitting, crawling, standing, and walking. In stage 2, young children develop more complex motor patterns (B), like running, climbing, jumping, balancing, catching, and throwing. In stage 3, older children develop greater automaticity and fluidity in performing the stage 2 motor patterns (C) while learning more specific movement skills. In stage 4, adolescents master specialized movements while ability, motivation, and practice influence continuing general and specific motor skills development (D).

49. D: Body mass index is the most widely used body composition measure that predicts or estimates body fat composition using the formula [weight in kg/ (height in m)^2]. Skinfold calipers measure skinfold thickness to estimate the percentage body fat. Hydrostatic weighing is a direct measure of body fat by comparing weight on land and the amount of water displaced by the body when submerged. Waist circumference is an estimated body fat measure that takes into account only the circumference of the waist.

50. A: Ari can help keep the ball inbounds by adding topspin, which will cause the ball to drop downward instead of going out of bounds. This is achieved by moving the striking arm from low to high with follow-through over the opposite shoulder. Increasing the speed of the racket may result in the ball traveling farther out. Stroke technique and contact point are more impactful than the amount of power placed on the ball.

51. C: A physiological benefit of exercise is it lowers the release of cortisol–a stress hormone and increases the release of endorphins–happy hormones. These physiological responses promote psychological outcomes or benefits including improved mood, positive thoughts, and increased confidence. Confidence also results from seeing the physical changes the body goes through from engaging in exercise.

52. D: Bandura's social learning theory is also known as observational learning theory, where watching someone's performance through modeling and demonstration as well as receiving feedback impact learning. Learning through touch, reading, and mental imagery also aid in learning but are not a part of observational learning theory.

53. D: The student lacks buoyancy and can fill up their lungs with air to help keep them afloat. Emptying the air in the lungs will decrease buoyancy and cause the student to sink. Drag slows down a swimmer and can be caused by wearing clothes or when the body is not in a streamlined position.

54. B: Skeletal muscles are responsible for muscle contraction and voluntary movements. The sliding filament theory (D) is the widely accepted theory that explains the process of concentric muscular contractions. Smooth muscles (A) are involuntary and responsible for intestinal contractions to help transport food throughout the body. Cardiac muscles (C) are also involuntary and are muscles of the heart responsible for contractions in the heart.

55. D: Max's hips are not far back enough during his squat, causing him to lose balance or stability. The heels should be flat as squatting on the toes can also create a forward motion. At one time, deep squats below 90 degrees were frowned upon, but new research indicates that a deep squat performed correctly is safe and does not impact balance. Max is likely to fall back if the chest is too low, which puts more weight in the rear, thus pulling him backward. A lifted chest with the hips back counters this effect.

56. C: Self-assessment allows students to take ownership of their learning and fosters intrinsic motivation to learn and engage in physical activities for a lifetime. Grades are extrinsic motivators and have less impact on learning and physical activity engagement. Fitness testing studies show that a large percentage of students dislike fitness testing. Self-assessment of fitness has been shown to be more effective than fitness testing. Ability tracking is what a teacher may do to plan for appropriate instruction, as same-ability grouping has shown the most effective in games and moderate to vigorous physical activity engagement.

57. D: PE classes must have a working cell phone or other communication device, regardless whether the equipment installation is in the school or elsewhere (a); the same applies to having a fully stocked, easily accessible first aid kit (b). Climbing ropes must also be compatible with the planned climbing activity and the belay device selected; these are NOT all compatible (c). Equipment must be manufactured specifically for the activity planned, and meet uniform standards (d).

58. B: Motive force is how much a lever can move an object; resistive force is how much resistance the object has against being moved by the lever. In the MA ratio, if the quotient is more than 1, resistive force is greater than motive force, not less (d). If the quotient is less than 1, motive force exceeds resistive force, not vice versa (a). If the quotient equals 1, there is NO advantage (c).

59. A: Students need more extrinsic (external) feedback from teachers or coaches when learning new PE skills. When they are more competent and confident with certain PE skills, they can analyze their own performance and make use of this intrinsic (internal) feedback. Choice (b) has this backwards. Students need both positive feedback for reinforcement and encouragement and negative feedback for correction (c), and both constructive and corrective (d) feedback, at all learning stages.

60. D: Jason has difficulty with kinesthetic discrimination, which requires identifying small movements in large gross motor activities. These are small movements of gross motor muscle groups and not fine motor movements with the hands and feet. Auditory discrimination is the ability to distinguish between sounds that are important and unimportant. Visual discrimination is the ability to distinguish objects, colors, shapes, and sizes.

61. C: Heart rate monitors are tools used to monitor heart rate and cardiovascular fitness intensity, which students can use and track over time. Having a low resting, exercise, and recovery heart rate suggest a good level of cardiovascular fitness. A lower resting, exercise, and recovery heart rate over time suggests improvement in cardiovascular fitness. Students can also use pedometers or step counters to track their steps with a widely accepted health goal of 10,000 steps a day. An increase in step count over time suggests an improvement in activity, but it cannot definitively determine fitness level. Calorie counters track the number of calories consumed for weight loss, maintenance, or weight gain, but they are not a fitness measure. Journal entries and reflections allow students to describe their experiences, including how they feel, e.g., "I am no longer out of breath when I walk up a flight of stairs," but are not objective tools to assess fitness levels.

62. D: Exploring the basics of these skills (a) most applies to students in grades K-2. Demonstrating mature forms of these skills (b) most applies to students in grades 3-5. Applying those mature forms in more specialized PE areas (c) most applies to students in grades 6-8. Using these motor skills for activities in these areas (d) most applies to students in grades 9-12.

63. C: The teacher should make sure that the standards were covered with padding to reduce the risk of liability as it is a foreseeable risk. It is not the teacher's responsibility to tie a student's shoes, but if the teacher notices that a student's shoelaces are untied, she should inform the student to tie them or tie them if the student does not know how. The student tripping over the shoelaces was an accident, but if the standards are uncovered, the teacher may be held liable for an injury. Safety rules rather than potential risks should be posted.

64. D: Modifying activities ensures equality in participation, learning, and succeeding in physical education. Activities can be modified by making skill activities easier for beginners and increasing skill challenges for advanced learners. Other modifications include increasing or decreasing time in activities, and varying distances, objects, targets, and boundaries. Recording teaching sessions will allow the teacher to evaluate if equity goals are met. Inviting administrators can provide feedback on equity, but it is not a physical education technique the ensures equal opportunities. Parents, unless educators or equity experts, are not in positions to evaluate teacher effectiveness. Parents may, however, observe a class to ensure that their child is being treated fairly. Appointing student captains is a technique used in physical education settings but does not ensure equal opportunities for students.

65. D: In a typical school PE risk management plan, General Supervisory Practices includes subcategories of Risk Management Planning Dimensions; Management of Student Behavior (C) / Rules and Regulations; Security; and <u>Care of Injured and Emergency Procedures</u>. Conduct of Activities and Services (A) includes Adequacy of Instruction and Progress; Use of Warnings and Participation Forms; Maturity and Condition of Participants; and Transportation of Students. Environmental Conditions (B) includes Equipment; Facility Layout; Area and Facility Maintenance; and Health Hazards.

66. D: The Federal Education Records and Privacy Act (FERPA) is the law that protects students' medical and personal information from dissemination without parental and/or children's consent. Individuals with Disabilities Education Act (IDEA) is a law that ensures that students with disabilities receive a quality education that includes providing appropriate accommodations for student success. Attention Deficit Hyperactivity Disorder (ADHD) is a mental health condition where individuals have difficulty focusing that is accompanied by hyperactive behaviors that can impede learning. The Health Insurance Portability and Accountability Act (HIPAA) is a law that protects patient privacy of medical information.

67. C: Activities that require agility and lower-body strength, which do not involve body contact (A), are most appropriate for coed participation and are less dependent on team assignment by student skill levels. For activities that require more upper-body strength (B), it is more important for physical education teachers to assign teams according to individual student skill levels to prevent injuries. Therefore, (D) is incorrect.

68. D: Students using wheelchairs need their hands to propel them (or press buttons or switches controlling power chairs) and cannot dribble a ball simultaneously, so letting them hold the ball in their laps while traveling is an adaptation. Using a "beeper ball" (a), putting a radio under the basket (b), and removing small obstacles from the court (c) are all basketball adaptations for students with visual impairments.

69. C: A BMI of 18.5 to 24.9 is classified as a normal, healthy proportion of body fat to height and weight. A BMI of 18.5 or lower (a) is considered underweight, i.e., insufficient body fat. A BMI of 25.0 to 29.9 (c) is classified as overweight, i.e., excessive body fat. A BMI of 30 or higher (d) is classified as obese, i.e., extremely excessive body fat.

70. B: Currently, experts recommend that children and adults aim to get 30 minutes per day of physical activity at a moderate intensity. For those whose schedules make this difficult, an alternative recommendation is for children to be moderately active in 5- to 10-minute sessions that add up to 60 minutes per day, and teens and adults to accumulate such session to at least 30 minutes per day.

71. B: Experts report that aerobic exercise can both elevate and stabilize mood (A); improve both sleep quality and self-esteem (B); reduce anxiety, even if the exercise is for as little as five minutes (C); improve concentration, alertness, and overall cognitive function, AND reduce fatigue (D). They recommend exercise not only for its physical benefits but also its mental fitness benefits, including reducing stress.

72. B: A PE teacher can use an app by showing video of professional athletes performing skills the students are learning (a) for demonstrating exemplary technique; showing video of classmates to identify not only errors (c) but also strengths for peer assessment or peer coaching; showing video at the end of a lesson (d) for teaching on the playing field and planning future lessons; and showing students video of their activity to identify their own strengths and needs for development (b) for analyzing their performance and progress.

73. A: Vicarious learning experiences, or watching others perform, helps build confidence and self-efficacy. Team cohesion is getting along with teammates to accomplish a common goal and may not directly impact self-efficacy, for example, a student who supports the team or is the team cheerleader but seldom plays during the game. The goal is to get the player to believe they can perform skills required during gameplay, so isolation learning does not include the environmental variables such as defenders, teammates, or time involved during gameplay. Respecting students is a contractual expectation of a teacher or coach.

74. C: Using a stopwatch or clock timer is an appropriate measure of duration or time engaged in aerobic activities for large classes. Pedometers are quick, easy, low-tech activity trackers that measure step count but do not measure duration (B). Pedometers and other activity trackers, e.g., Fitbits or Polar HR monitors, can waste instructional time and be expensive (A). There also may not be enough pedometers or activity trackers to use for large classes. Aerobic equipment, including treadmills, ellipticals, cycles, and rowing machines have timers; however, there usually are not enough for all students to use simultaneously(D).

75. B: The student has not developed emotional self-regulation, which is the ability to control emotions, usually developed by age six. Emotional knowledge is recognizing the emotional state of another. Self-efficacy is the personal belief or confidence in performing a skill. Self-esteem is how one feels about themselves, which can be high/positive or low/negative.

76. C: Elective physical education programs allow students to decide or choose the type of programming. Student choice has been shown to increase student motivation. More focus on students' strengths rather than the teacher's strengths is also a benefit. Equipment is dependent on a budget, but some elective programs might be driven by equipment availability. Equipment, however, should not guide the curriculum or course offerings. Physical education is a part of a holistic educational experience, and the goal is to develop students, not provide scheduling relief.

77. C: Training at a percentage of the maximum heart rate (MHR) is used to assess heart rate intensity during exercise. For cardiovascular fitness, working at 65 to 85% of the MHR is the recommended range, with beginners starting at the lower limits and advanced exercisers working at the upper limits. Elite endurance athletes or those with high cardiovascular fitness can work at 90% of MHR. Continuous aerobic activity is a method to determine the time and/or distance of the activity. The talk test aids in determining relative intensity based on if one can or cannot talk or sing during cardiovascular activities. If one is unable to talk, the intensity is too high for continuous activity. If one can talk but not sing, the intensity is at a moderate level. If they can sing, the intensity is too low. Recovery heart rate is the time it takes for the heart to return to normal or rest after activity and is one way to measure cardiovascular improvements. The fitter one becomes, the faster the heart rate returns to normal.

78. B: The spectators demonstrated poor etiquette or unwritten expectations of behavior that ensure a healthy and safe environment for participants and observers. Unsportsmanlike behaviors are reserved for the participants. Rule violations are restricted to each sport, activity, or facility space and may be committed by players, coaches, or spectators. Spectator violations are classified as written or posted rule violations, such as no food or drink in the gym.

79. B: The PE teacher should first check the scene for safety. Next, she would check the spectator for signs of consciousness, e.g., talking, breathing, and pulse. If there is no breathing, the PE teacher would identify and instruct someone to call 911 and include the assessment. If there is an AED available, that request would also be made followed by CPR until the AED arrives, medical personnel arrive, and/or the PE teacher is too tired to continue performing CPR correctly.

80. C: The President's Council on Physical Fitness and Sports identifies "Fundamental Building Blocks" for using PE to promote positive student development. The structure of these is that giving opportunities and access to PA for all young people enables establishing ideal contexts for engaging in PA, which in turn allows PE educators to help students attain developmental health outcomes.

81. A: Heart rate monitors detect the speed or rate that the heart beats and determines exercise intensity. An accelerometer is a tracking device that can inform the teacher of students' acceleration or speed changes since acceleration is a change in speed. Pedometers are step counters that track the number of steps taken. Some fitness tracking devices include all of the above as well as sleep, sitting, and minutes engaged in physical activity.

82. B: Bodyweight exercises are recommended for beginning students in weight training. Bodyweight exercises reduce the risk of injury and teach students how to move the body for physiological adaptations. After bodyweight exercises, light weights, including dumbbells, are introduced with gradual increases in weight. Students are often directed to select a light weight and perform a few reps and, if too easy, select a heavier weight in small increments until the last two or three reps in an 8-to-15-rep count are challenging. This can be used to conduct a predicted one-repetition max test by using predicted one-rep max calculators. The one-repetition max strength test is not appropriate for physical education as lifting the heaviest amount possible in one-rep increases injury risk. Alternating between light and heavy weight is a training method for muscular strength and endurance goals but is not employed with beginners.

83. A: Partner activities focus on relationships with others. While leading and following are partner activities, these are under the "relationship with others" movement concept. Partner activities are the normal progression before participating in larger team activities but are not movement concepts. High and low levels can also be taught in pairs but are subcomponents of the movement concept spatial awareness.

84. C: Both verbal and nonverbal feedback aid in student learning and are more effective when used together. The effectiveness of each type of feedback is dependent on the learning style of students. For auditory learners, verbal feedback may be more effective, and for visual learners, nonverbal feedback may be best. Combining verbal, nonverbal, and kinesthetic feedback is ideal, as these accommodate diverse learners.

85. D: Differentiation is a strategy that addresses multiple abilities that exist in one class. The teacher should have activities for beginner, intermediate, and advanced students to meet all learners' needs and include extensions and remediations. Some students have mastered or exceeded the learning outcome but still need to be challenged and learn new ways of doing things.

86. D: The teacher should vary the sizes of the balls thrown as students may not be able to grip the balls used. Having students throw to each other is no different than throwing at a target, and if positioned at the same distance, the ball will still not reach. Keeping the targets in place does not solve the problem. Reviewing skill cues is appropriate, but skill cues are not modifications of the task.

87. D: The Society for Health and Physical Educators (SHAPE) America sets the national K-12 and physical education teacher education standards. The Council for the Accreditation of Educator Preparation (CAEP) is responsible for accreditation of physical education teacher education programs and working closely with SHAPE America. GOPHER is the largest equipment supplier for physical education and has partnered with SHAPE America. The former National Association of Sport and Physical Education (NASPE) is now SHAPE after combining with the American Alliance for Health, Physical Education, Recreation and Dance.

88. A: Eating a high carbohydrate meal, also known as carb loading, before an endurance activity is done for fast and easy recruitment of glucose and glycogen energy rather than waiting 20-minutes for the fat energy stores to become available, which could slow down a runner's pace. If running on an empty stomach, the body will need to recruit stored glucose (glycogen). While glycogen is a faster energy source than fats, glucose obtained from a light snack or breakfast is more ideal as it is already in the bloodstream and does not need to metabolize or be broken down like glycogen and stored fat. The meal is equitable but that is not the most important reason for eating a high carbohydrate meal before an endurance activity. Depending on the time the meal is eaten, it may help or hurt sleep, but it is not the purpose of carb loading.

89. B: The teacher is promoting diversity among students as the students' dance preferences are influenced by the students' cultures. Since the students submitted dances at the beginning of the school year, this is not an example of choice. Choice would indicate that the students choose the dance for the day or week, but in this scenario, the teacher is randomly choosing from student submissions. Self-efficacy is the belief that one can perform a skill or task. Autonomy is the freedom and independence to make choices on one's behalf. An example of autonomy in physical education is the freedom to move and choose activities as illustrated in creative movement activities, including dance.

90. B: Variable practice has been shown to be the most effective in PE and sport settings, as the same game skills are practiced in various situations to mimic real play, e.g., small-sided games. Random practice is mixing up skills in random order, which is similar to variable practice, but the skills differ. Blocked practice focuses on one skill at a time and repeats, which is evident during isolation skills practice. Mental practice is thinking about or rehearsing the skill cognitively, which has been shown to benefit physical skills when used in conjunction with physical practice, but it is not as strong when used independently.

Constructed Response

91. This is the rubric used to score constructed-response questions on the CSET.

Purpose	The extent to which the response addresses the constructed-response assignment's charge in relation to relevant CSET content specifications or subject matter requirements.
Subject Matter Knowledge	Application of accurate subject matter knowledge as described in the relevant CSET content specifications or subject matter requirements.
Support	The appropriateness and quality of the supporting evidence in relation to relevant CSET content specifications or subject matter requirements.

Score Point	Score Point Description
3	**The "3" response reflects command of the relevant knowledge and skills as defined in the CSET content specifications or subject matter requirements.** • The purpose of the assignment is fully achieved. • There is an accurate application of relevant content specifications or subject matter requirements. • There is appropriate and specific relevant supporting evidence.
2	**The "2" response reflects general command of the relevant knowledge and skills as defined in the CSET content specifications or subject matter requirements.** • The purpose of the assignment is largely achieved. • There is a largely accurate application of relevant content specifications or subject matter requirements. • There is acceptable relevant supporting evidence.
1	**The "1" response reflects limited or no command of the relevant knowledge and skills as defined in the CSET content specifications or subject matter requirements.** • The purpose of the assignment is only partially or not achieved. • There is limited or no application of relevant content specifications or subject matter requirements. • There is little or no relevant supporting evidence.
U	**The "U" (unscorable) is assigned to a response that is unrelated to the assignment, illegible, primarily in a language other than English, or does not contain a sufficient amount of original work to score.**
B	**The "B" (blank) is assigned to a response that is blank.**

Practice Test #2

Multiple Choice Questions

1. In creating a positive climate for PE student learning activities, which of the following accurately reflects an expert recommendation or principle?

a. Increasing learning opportunities creates a positive climate.
b. Teachers must use a few motivational strategies uniformly.
c. Students must already have learned appropriate behaviors.
d. Holding students accountable destroys the positive climate.

2. Which of the following is an example of metabolic syndrome related to sedentary lifestyles?

a. Heart disease and overactive thyroid
b. High cholesterol, hypertension, and obesity
c. Hypokinetic disease and physical inactivity
d. Obesity, low blood glucose, and diabetes

3. Of the following, which best describes high school learning standards for balance skills in PE?

a. Utilizing dynamic balance for transitions in gymnastics, between sport movements
b. Creating and showing a balance sequence using counterbalances, counter-tensions
c. Demonstrating a variety of static and dynamic balance, either singly or with others
d. Demonstrating static balance with different body parts, shapes, and support bases

4. Divers and skaters can control the speed of their turns through the length of the rotation radius around the center of gravity. Relative to this biomechanical principle, which choice is true?

a. The body turns less slowly with arms extended.
b. The body turns most slowly in the pike position.
c. The body turns most slowly in full tuck position.
d. The body turns most slowly in lay-out position.

5. What accurately represents a difference between aerobic dance and ballet or jazz dance classes?

a. Aerobic dance is the only one that raises the heart rates for students.
b. Aerobic dance is the only one that sustains continual student motion.
c. Aerobic dance is the only one that increases student respiration rates.
d. Aerobic dance is the only one that augments the perspiration volume.

6. Some students with obese body mass indices are reluctant to participate during the fitness activities but are actively engaged in team sports as indicated on their heart rate monitors during game play. Which of the following can the teacher do to increase fitness participation among these students?

a. focus on health
b. focus on standards
c. focus on competitive fitness activities
d. focus on body composition

7. Of these, which one is classified as a locomotor skill?

a. Hopping
b. Bending
c. Twisting
d. Turning

8. Which of the following is a defensive running pattern common in dual and team sports?

a. high level
b. zigzags
c. transitions
d. curves

9. Josh has started to grasp the follow-through motion during his jump shots, which he was unable to demonstrate at the beginning of the unit. Which of the following best describes Josh's stage of learning?

a. Beginner
b. Associative
c. Autonomous
d. Advanced

10. A bowler is capable of hitting the middle pin relatively consistently. What is one way they can improve their success at making strikes?

a. Using a heavier ball
b. Moving further to the left
c. Putting more spin on the ball
d. Throwing the ball from farther away

11. Which of the following curriculum approaches focuses on the fundamental movement skills needed for advanced movement skills in sport and physical activities over the lifespan?

a. Sport Education
b. Teaching Games for Understanding
c. Skill Themes
d. Cooperative Learning

12. Which intensity of aerobic exercise have researchers found provides the greatest protection to the cardiovascular system against coronary heart disease specifically?

a. Mild intensity
b. Vigorous intensity
c. Moderate intensity
d. Any level of intensity

13. Which of the following best describes the appropriate duration training for a midfielder in soccer?

a. Long duration
b. Short duration
c. Intervals
d. Player specific

14. A PE teacher evaluates student performance in archery by measuring student accuracy in hitting a standardized target from a specified distance. This represents which kind of assessment?

a. Norm-referenced
b. Process assessment
c. Criterion-referenced
d. Biomechanical objectives

15. Why is it important for individuals to know the health history of their parents prior to engaging in physical activity?

a. Predisposed health conditions
b. Previous musculoskeletal injuries
c. Effects of physical activity response
d. Physical activity readiness questionnaire

16. In a PE class, which of these would be an example of descriptive feedback?

a. "Wow, great form!"
b. "Stand sideways!"
c. "Use your instep!"
d. "Follow through!"

17. Several students are focused only on training their abdominal muscles to reduce belly fat. What is the best advice to provide students to maximize their outcomes?

a. Make sure to work antagonist core muscles
b. Increase the intensity of abdominal workouts
c. Train the abdominals every other day
d. Vary the workouts

18. PE teachers who collect and interpret more student data than just fitness scores can use these data to do which of the following?

a. To show they are teaching, regardless of whether students are learning
b. To show what students should practice, not what they already know
c. To show which students need more help, not those making progress
d. To show parents, principals, school boards the value of PE programs

19. Which of the following is an example of a psychological approach that aims to develop intrinsic student motivation in physical education?

a. Self-determination theory
b. Behaviorism theory
c. Social theory
d. Constructivism theory

20. Carlos is at a healthy weight for his age and gender. Which of the following best depicts the energy balance equation that Carlos should employ to maintain a healthy weight?

a. Energy in ≠ energy out
b. Energy in < energy out
c. Energy in > energy out
d. Energy in = energy out

21. Which of the following indicates an effective muscular endurance training program?

a. Increasing the rep count over time
b. Increasing soreness over time
c. Maintaining the rep count over time
d. Increasing the weight over time

22. Which of the following agencies set the goals and curricula for state-level K-12 physical education?

a. SHAPE
b. CAEP
c. HPE
d. ESSA

23. Which of the following distinguishes etiquette between individual and team sports?

a. personal vs. team fouls
b. no coaching vs. coaching
c. no noise vs. loud noise
d. no penalty cards vs. yellow and red cards

24. Which of the following best contrasts perceptual motor abilities and physical proficiency abilities?

a. Muscular endurance and muscular strength
b. Reaction time and control precision
c. Reaction time and muscular strength
d. Control precision and finger dexterity

25. In which of the following school levels is movement education most appropriate?

a. Pre-kindergarten
b. Elementary school
c. Middle school
d. High school

26. Excess body fat increases the risk of poor health. Which of the following activities aids in establishing a healthy body composition?

a. Increase physical activity when eating foods with fat
b. Avoid foods with fat
c. Cross-train and monitor food intake
d. Read food labels and move more

27. Students in class have a cross country meet tomorrow. Which of the following recommendations will help students prepare?

a. "Take a practice run on the course."
b. "Take a practice run at a lower intensity."
c. "Get more rest and increase fat intake."
d. "Get more rest and increase carbohydrate intake."

28. Katherine wants to train her shoulders and neck for swim season. Which of the following exercises will meet Katherine's needs?

a. Lateral deltoid raises and shrugs
b. Shoulder curls and deltoid raises
c. Deltoid curls and shrugs
d. Anterior and rear deltoid raises

29. The teacher has set up a circuit for students to engage in health-related fitness activities including muscular strength and endurance. Which of the following training measures should the teacher address to ensure safety?

a. progressive overload
b. specificity
c. regression
d. spotting

30. Which of the following describes how dances aid in development of respect for diversity?

a. Every student can participate
b. Every student's culture can be included
c. Every locomotor movement can be used
d. Every non-locomotor movement can be used

31. Which of the following describes the knowledge of *performance* vs. knowledge of *results*?

a. Intrinsic vs. extrinsic feedback
b. Extrinsic vs. intrinsic feedback
c. Performance feedback vs. intrinsic feedback
d. Extrinsic feedback vs. performance feedback

32. Justice is in grade 9 and shares with the PE teacher that he read in a muscle magazine that he should weight train one muscle group a week to increase muscle size but he is not seeing any results. Which of the following is an appropriate response?

a. "Wait for puberty."
b. "Refrain from doing cardio activities."
c. "Hypertrophy is an unrealistic goal."
d. "Try cross-training."

33. Research finds cooperative learning beneficial across school subjects. It is particularly applicable to PE, which involves a high proportion of team and small-group activities. Which component of cooperative learning entails student reflection on group or team progress toward learning goals?

a. Social skills
b. Group processing
c. Individual accountability
d. Positive interdependence

34. Which of the following explains the importance of discipline when engaging in recreational activities?

a. The rules of engagement are unclear.
b. There is no one to monitor activity.
c. The outcome goals are unclear.
d. Goals vary for each individual.

35. Which of the following is an example of integrated physical education?

a. Allowing students to choose curricula that relate to classroom content
b. Having students analyze the angles of underhand and overhand throws
c. Inviting specialists to cover topics such as yoga
d. Inviting classroom teachers to teach concepts

36. What is true about legal requirements for proving negligence, as applied to a PE teacher?

a. The PE teacher must have had a duty to meet a certain standard of conduct.
b. The PE teacher need not have breached his or her duty to be found negligent.
c. The PE teacher must have been the actual but not proximate cause of injury.
d. The PE teacher need not have caused actual damages to be found negligent.

37. Among the major body systems, which types of muscles produce voluntary movement?

a. Skeletal muscles
b. Smooth muscles
c. Both these types
d. Neither of these

38. A physical education program has a 4:1 student-equipment ratio, a large teaching area, a class size of 38-42 students, and students are engaged at least 50% of the time. Which of the following elements of an effective physical education program is present and appropriately accounted for in the example?

a. equipment ratio and teaching area
b. class size and student engagement
c. student engagement and equipment ratio
d. student engagement and teaching area

39. Coach Wheelock refuses to let the girls on the school's basketball team play with the boys in physical education because he says the boys play too rough. Which of the following practices does Coach Wheelock exhibit?

a. Safety for injury prevention
b. Gender discrimination
c. Favoritism towards the boys
d. Gender stereotypes

40. The teacher would like to teach the movement concepts effort, relationships, and spatial awareness. Which of the following activities are recommended to develop these concepts?

a. Stationary movements
b. Balancing on the balance beam
c. Fitness activities
d. Animal walks

41. Regarding appropriate physical education (PE) teaching practices, which statement is MOST valid?

a. PE teachers must use extrinsic motivations to teach student responsibility for learning.
b. PE teachers should ignore certain inappropriate student behaviors to extinguish them.
c. PE teachers do not necessarily need to obtain or renew certification in cardiopulmonary resuscitation (CPR) or automated external defibrillator (AED) use.
d. PE teachers must regularly and consistently inspect facilities and equipment for safety.

42. Which of the following high school trends have impacted the shift away from team sports to health-related fitness in physical education programs?

a. technology
b. childhood obesity
c. adult preparation
d. health promotion

43. Which of the following is a strategy used for refinement of manipulative skills?

a. tag games
b. increased opportunities to respond
c. leading and following a peer
d. choice of manipulative skill

44. Recent trends and philosophies about PE and its role in both encouraging physical activity (PA) and using it to promote positive student development include which of the following?

a. Children and teens are resources for developing competencies.
b. Children and teens are problems that adults need to manage.
c. Physical activity promotes health, not happiness, for Americans.
d. Only educators can use PA to optimize development for youth.

45. Which of the following fitness activities are students engaged in when participating in orienteering?

a. Walking, hiking, and swimming
b. Walking, cycling, and swimming
c. Walking, jogging, and running
d. Swimming, cycling, and running

46. Students and others who are obese, or are overweight and have two or more other risk factors, can decrease their risk of developing related diseases by losing how much of their existing body weight?

a. 5-10 percent
b. 15-20 percent
c. 25-30 percent
d. 35-40 percent

47. Which of the following methods would be LEAST useful for assessing student performance of physical education skills?

a. Observational checklists
b. Rating scales of skill level
c. Written-response exams
d. Performance data graphs

48. Michael, a 15-year-old student, has the appearance of working at a high intensity (heavy breathing, perspiring) but his heart rate monitor is consistent at 72 bpm. The teacher assigns another heart rate monitor to check for accuracy and the heart rate remains at 72 bpm. Which of the following should occur next?

a. stopping him from exercising
b. allowing him to continue exercising
c. conducting a talk test with him
d. taking his blood pressure

49. Which of the following is a good explanation of why several students throughout the school year have contracted bacterial infections after physical education classes?

a. coughing with their mouths open
b. engaging in skin-to-skin contact
c. rolling around on mats
d. failing to shower after class

50. Of the following beliefs common among high school students about exercise, nutrition, and health, which is accurate rather than a misconception or myth?

a. Eat simple carbs after exercising.
b. Everybody should take vitamins.
c. Drink eight glasses of water per day.
d. Vitamins supply greater energy.

51. Among basic body positions, which of these do many movement stunts pass through, begin with, or end with most often?

a. Sit
b. Pike
c. Tuck
d. Straddle

52. Several students walk with rounded shoulders or hunched backs. Which of the following exercises will foster good posture and flexibility?

a. curl-ups
b. back extensions
c. pectorals deck
d. lateral raises

53. Which of the following steps used in jazz dance is similar to the gallop?

a. chasse
b. axel
c. ball change
d. the drop

54. Which of the following safety measures are the responsibility of the teacher?

a. posting the safety rules in the gym
b. posting a link to the school-wide safety plan
c. posting the emergency exit protocols
d. posting fire drill protocols

55. The teacher overhears a student express shock that the large-statured classmate had higher cardiovascular results than all of the smaller-statured athletes in class. Which of the following concepts does the teacher need to teach or re-teach?

a. The difference between body fat and health
b. The difference between body composition and height
c. The difference between body size and fitness
d. The difference between fitness and health

56. Students in grades 9-12 should be able to do which of these with manipulative motor skills?

a. Refining and applying complex manipulative skills in lead-up games
b. Creating advanced movement skills and demonstrating using them
c. Demonstrating progress toward more manipulative skill complexity
d. Applying basic and advanced skills to sports, dance, and gymnastics

57. Jennifer, a student with visual impairment, has difficulty seeing the colors on the archery targets. Which type of adaption should the teacher consider?

a. a task-specific adaptation
b. an equipment-specific adaption
c. a boundary-specific adaptation
d. a task and boundary-specific adaptation

58. Which of the following is an example of a SHAPE America grade level outcome?

a. The student will recognize value in physical activity
b. The student will demonstrate motor skills
c. The student will apply movement concepts
d. The student will skip using a mature pattern

59. The teacher has little time to go over each health-related fitness component in isolation. Which of the following activities can the teacher use to implement the health-related fitness components when short on time?

a. resistance training
b. interval training
c. fartlek training
d. circuit training

60. The President's Council on Physical Fitness and Sports (2009) identifies five levels of responsibility as positive youth development goals, including the choices below. Of these, which is most related to the self-management skill of self-direction?

a. Respecting the feelings and rights of others
b. Trying out new tasks and persisting at tasks
c. Independent work, progressive goal setting
d. Democratic approaches to resolving conflict

61. Which of the following is correct regarding principles of aerobic exercise?

a. Aerobic exercise involves small muscle groups.
b. Aerobic exercise entails continuous movement.
c. Aerobic exercise will firm and tone the muscles.
d. Aerobic exercise burns fat only at low intensity.

62. A PE teacher or coach responds to different student learning styles when teaching new movement or sport skills. Which of these instructional strategies would best help a student with a mainly verbal learning style?

a. The teacher or coach gives a demonstration of the skill to imitate.
b. The teacher or coach adds a diagram of the skill to demonstration.
c. The teacher or coach guides students through demonstrated skills.
d. The teacher or coach explains the skill aloud during demonstration.

63. Which statement is correct regarding apparatus and procedures for testing sports equipment, specifically helmets?

a. Auto crash simulation headforms are used to test linear impact from head collisions in football.
b. Drop towers for testing helmet impact performance also apply with head collisions in football.
c. The stretch in a helmet retention system is tested the same as the retention system's strength.
d. The mouthguard on a helmet is designed to protect the teeth, not the brain from a concussion.

64. Where should a sprinter's center of gravity be to accelerate fastest out of the starting block?

a. It should be as high as possible.
b. It should be as low as possible.
c. It should be right in the middle.
d. It should be a full upright body.

65. Which of the following best describes the model used in physical education that incorporates biomechanics and Physics during the throwing unit?

a. physical education and sport science
b. integrated physical education
c. exercise and sport science
d. kinesiology

66. The teacher has planned a hiking unit to take advantage of the neighboring hiking trails. Which of the following is a procedural issue that should be employed?

a. Applying sunscreen
b. Assigning a student-leader
c. Charging the teacher's cell phone
d. Taking attendance

67. At the beginning of the semester, a student had a resting heart rate of 72 bpm, and by the end of the unit, the resting heart rate was 82 bpm. Which of the following best explains the change in heart rate?

a. An increase in fitness
b. A decrease in fitness
c. Heart disease
d. Tachycardia

68. Which of the following stretching practices has shown to have the greatest improvements in flexibility?

a. active stretching
b. PNF stretching
c. ballistic stretching
d. dynamic stretching

69. Jacquan would like to create a weight management program that helps him lose weight. Which of the following would help Jacquan reach his goal?

a. Energy homeostasis
b. Energy imbalance
c. Energy balance
d. Energy drinks

70. Callie slips on the spilled water on the gym floor and breaks her arm during physical education class. Which of the following violations has occurred?

a. Accountability
b. Misfeasance
c. Negligence
d. Malfeasance

71. Among movement skill competencies reflecting developmental standards, which is most suitable for students in the fifth grade?

a. Moving creatively to varied musical rhythms using simple dance steps
b. Jumping rope to the tempo of music, both singly and with a partner
c. Bouncing, passing, and catching a ball, matching a musical rhythm
d. Expressing feelings, ideas in rhythmic motion with, without music

72. Basic principles of physical fitness include Overload and FITT. When combining these two, which of the following can be changed for BOTH resistance (weight) training AND cardiovascular (aerobic) training?

a. Changing the workout by doing different exercises
b. Increasing the number of repetitions to complete
c. Increasing the resistance or weight being pressed
d. Increasing the number of days when working out

73. Which of the following manipulative skills is NOT classified as propulsive?

a. Kicking
b. Striking
c. Catching
d. Throwing

74. Which of the following exercises targets the abdominal muscles?

a. Air bicycle
b. Alien squat
c. Axle deadlift
d. Dumbbell curl

75. The teacher observes students daily and compares movement to the skill cues or model to provide student feedback. Which assessment strategy is the teacher using?

a. Formative assessment
b. Summative assessment
c. Assessment for learning
d. Assessment as learning

76. According to social learning theorist Albert Bandura, which of the following factors that influence observational learning most involves practicing kinesthetic and neuromuscular patterns repeatedly to imitate the teacher or other model's demonstration?

a. Attention
b. Retention
c. Reproduction
d. Reinforcement

77. Which of the following activities improve flexibility and posture?

a. isometric training
b. plank exercises
c. free weight training
d. running

78. The teacher consistently provides direct verbal and demonstrative feedback to beginning students. What is the purpose of using these feedback strategies?

a. To diversify feedback delivery
b. To help students practice the desired outcome
c. To help students perfect the desired outcome
d. To help students understand the desired outcome

79. Kimberly is not demonstrating opposition during the overhand throw. Which of the following techniques will promote the desired outcome?

a. Telling her she needs to step with the opposite foot
b. Telling her to practice daily
c. Telling her to work with a partner
d. The teacher should recognize that all students will not master every skill and move on

80. Which of the following cardiovascular and endurance training risk-reduction steps can be used in physical education programs?

a. A PAR-Q
b. A talk test
c. A medical waiver
d. A warm-up

81. Student-centered instructional approaches have been shown to be more effective than teacher-driven approaches. Which of the following student-centered approaches has been shown to increase motivation?

a. Choice
b. Direct instruction
c. Competition
d. Traditional

82. Which of the following best describes the purpose of rhythmic activities?

a. To learn music tempo
b. To learn how to perform
c. To learn how to control the body
d. To learn the locomotor movements

83. Which of the following laws gives women and girls equal access to sports and education?

a. Title IX
b. Roe v. Wade
c. Women's Rights Act
d. The Civil Rights Act

84. Of these weight training exercises that use body weight rather than equipment, which kind is used to strengthen muscles in the torso?

a. Squats
b. Lunges
c. Planks
d. Bridges

85. Which of the following is the best training program to improve muscular endurance?

a. High weight, low reps
b. High weight, high reps
c. Low weight, low reps
d. Low weight, high reps

86. PE teachers must instruct students to monitor their heart rates during and after aerobic exercise. At what time should they instruct students to take their recovery heart rates?

a. After cooling down
b. Right after exercise
c. While cooling down
d. Between exercising

87. Which of the following best describes the role of balance in agility-based tasks?

a. Balance supports an athlete's stability when moving quickly.
b. Balance supports an athlete's ability to run fast.
c. Balance supports an athlete's ability to use multiple movement skills proficiently.
d. Balance supports an athlete's ability to quickly change directions.

88. Which of the following best explains the rationale behind physical education promoting physical activity over the lifespan?

a. Lowers the risk of heart disease
b. Increases blood pressure
c. Responsible for muscle atrophy
d. Decreases endorphins

89. Four developmental levels of student personal and social responsibility in PE have been identified (Hellison, 1995). To facilitate student growth by building on student strengths, at which level would it be appropriate for a PE teacher to use a peer teaching strategy to increase student interaction?

a. Level 1, self-control
b. Level 0, irresponsibility
c. Level 2, involvement
d. Level 4, caring

90. Regarding inherent risks of participating in some physical activities in a school PE program, school risk management plans typically include an Agreement to Participate form at the beginning of the school year, term, or semester. Which parties are typically required to sign this form?

a. Students and their parents or guardians
b. Only students' parents or guardians are
c. Only the students are required to sign it
d. Students, their parents, and PE teachers

Constructed Response

91. Use the graphic below to complete the exercise that follows.

USDA MyPlate

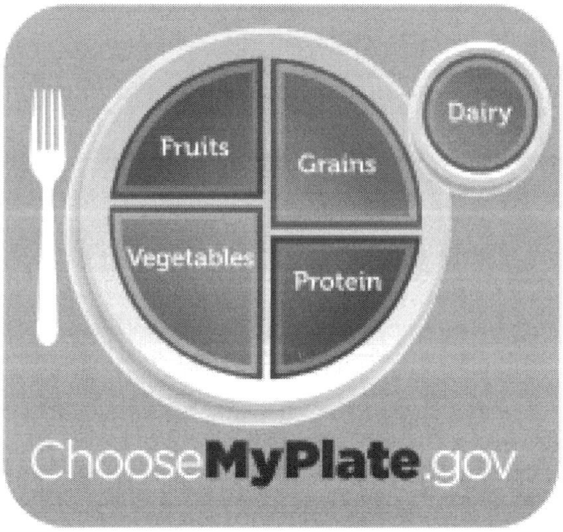

The USDA introduced the MyPlate graphic to provide guidance to Americans regarding healthy eating choices. Using your knowledge of childhood nutrition requirements:

- Create a daily meal plan for an 8-year-old child that aligns with the recommendations included in MyPlate.
- Identify one struggle that a parent or guardian may face while preparing and serving a meal aligned with the nutritional recommendations of MyPlate.
- Explain one solution that will encourage children to make healthy and nutritious food choices.

Answer Key and Explanations for Test #2

Multiple Choice Questions

1. A: Experts at PE Central say one way PE teachers can create a positive climate for student activity and learning is to increase the opportunities for students to learn. They also say creating this positive climate requires using many varied motivational strategies (b), helping students learn and sustain appropriate behaviors (c), and promoting student responsibility and accountability (d).

2. B: Metabolic syndrome is a medical condition related to sedentary lifestyles and poor nutritional habits that includes three or more risk factors including obesity, high cholesterol, hypertension (high blood pressure), high glucose (high blood sugar), and excessive fat around the waist. All of these factors occur in a cluster which increases the risk of diabetes, stroke, and heart disease. Hypokinetic diseases are also lifestyle conditions that result from inactivity or sedentary living that include the risk factors of metabolic syndrome as well as osteoarthritis, osteoporosis, some cancers, depression, and lower-back pain.

3. A: Students in grades 9-12 can be expected to utilize dynamic balance to make transitions in gymnastics routines and between movements in specific sports. Students in grades 6-8 can be expected to create a sequence of balances using counterbalances and counter-tensions, and to demonstrate this sequence (B). Students in grades 3-5 can be expected to demonstrate a variety of static and dynamic balances, by themselves or with others (C). Students in grades K-2 can be expected to demonstrate static balance using different body parts, shapes, and support bases (D).

4. D: The body will turn slowest with the greatest radius of rotation, and fastest with the smallest rotation radius. Extending the arms creates the longest radius; therefore, the body turns *more* slowly, not less, with arms extended (A). In the pike position, the body turns at a medium speed (B); pulling the arms in toward the body shortens the radius, causing faster rotation. So the body turns fastest in full tuck position (C), and slowest in lay-out position (D).

5. B: Apart from artistic and stylistic purposes, a main difference between aerobic and ballet or jazz dance is that ballet and jazz classes do not sustain continuous movement, so they are essentially not aerobic in nature. Stopping between exercises is frequent as teachers change music and identify, explain, and demonstrate each exercise. While all three dance forms raise heart rates (a), increase breathing rates (c), and make students sweat (d), aerobic dance classes are the only ones maintaining those elevated rates longer than several consecutive minutes.

6. C: For these students, achieving fitness through team sports is a more realistic goal. The teacher can employ competitive or team fitness activities where the focus is on a team goal rather than health, the standards, or body composition. Obese students tend to dislike physical education and physical activities due to bodies on display and the promotion of thinness or normal weight body mass indices, which are more pronounced during fitness activities. The teacher can provide instruction that promotes health and use the standards in a team-based approach, but doing so during traditional fitness activities may ostracize student engagement, especially when focusing on body composition.

7. A: Hopping is defined as jumping off and landing on a surface using the same foot. It is classified as a locomotor skill because it involves movement between or among points in space. Bending (B), twisting (C), and turning (D) are all classified as non-locomotor skills because they involve moving the body without changing position and little or no movement of the body's support base.

8. B: Zigzag running or alternating diagonal patterns are common in dual and team sports. Transitions occur in dual and team sports, but it is the transition from offense to defense and vice versa with footwork patterns differing across sport types. Curve patterns are not common in dual and team sports. Some team sports have high-level movements like jumping in volleyball and basketball, but dual sports such as tennis and badminton, use mostly medium-level movements but not defensive running patterns.

9. B: Josh is in the associative stage of Fitts and Posners' stages of motor learning, which is when the student starts to grasp the movement skill and relies less on the teacher or skill cues which are beginner behaviors. A student in the autonomous stage has internalized a skill thoroughly enough that they can perform it automatically, i.e., with minimal or no thought. Autonomous and advanced levels may be considered as the same stage, though "advanced" is not part of Fitts and Posners' model. A student capable of advanced performance is likely to be considered in the autonomous stage of motor learning.

10. A: The bowler should use a heavier ball for more power to knock down all of the pins. There is no need for the bowler to move left since the middle pin is struck consistently. Putting more spin on the ball would help the bowler achieve a strike if the pins were struck from the side rather than down the middle. The bowler will likely lose power if the ball is thrown from farther away.

11. C: The Skill Themes approach focuses on teaching the fundamental movement skills (e.g., catching and throwing; running and sliding) required to perform more complex movements needed for sport and leisure activities. Sport Education is an approach to teaching team sports where every student has a role, such as player, coach, referee, or scorekeeper, which changes when starting a new "season" or the next sport. Teaching Games for Understanding (TGfU) is a tactical approach to teaching team sports that involves creating an environment where students have to make decisions during gameplay. Cooperative learning is a student-centered approach where students work together towards a common goal. Cooperative learning activities are evident or can be implemented in many curriculum approaches including the ones aforementioned.

12. B: While even mild (A) exercise is better than none, and moderate (C) exercise prevents a great variety of illnesses, researchers have found aerobic exercise at a vigorous intensity level the most beneficial specifically to protect the cardiovascular system against coronary heart disease. Therefore, (D) is incorrect.

13. C: The appropriate training schedule for a midfielder in soccer is interval training with the Fartlek method of switching between random speeds consisting of short sprints, running downfield, walking, and jogging. These are helpful because movements in soccer can vary drastically. Long duration training is more appropriate for endurance activities including cross country and cycling. Short duration training is more appropriate for short or explosive activities, e.g., the 100-meter sprint and jumping. Duration training is specific to the game or position rather than the player.

14. D: A norm-referenced (a) assessment or standardized test evaluates basic PE skills objectively by comparing student results to those of a normative, representative student sample group. A process assessment (b) is a subjective approach, using observation to identify and correct errors in skill form, mechanics, or style. Product assessments (how fast/high/many/far) are quantitative, hence objective. A criterion-referenced (c) assessment evaluates PE skills against defined performance standards. PE teachers can also evaluate performance using biomechanical learning objectives (d) as in the example described.

15. A: Some medical conditions, such as hypertension, can be exacerbated by engaging in certain physical activities; therefore, it is important to know if participants are predisposed to or have hereditary health conditions to ensure a safe exercise environment. Musculoskeletal injuries are generally the result of overtraining, muscle overuse, awkward movements, colliding with a person or object, or are age-related, such as with osteoporosis.

16. A: Descriptive feedback, like choice A, provides feedback that describes what the student is currently doing. It can reinforce what the student is currently doing, but it does not attempt to correct an error. Each of the other answer choices are examples of prescriptive feedback, which helps students learn motor skills correctly by telling the student what to do or how to do it.

17. D: Spot training is not effective for weight loss, so students should vary their workouts. Students should work the entire body as fat cells shrink in multiple areas not controlled by the exerciser. Large muscle groups like the quadriceps, back, abs, and pectorals burn more fat. Eating a well-balanced, low-fat diet also aids in weight loss. Antagonist core muscles such as the erector spinae, rhomboids, and lats should be worked to keep a balanced body and reduce injury risk. Intensity can be increased by doing more abdominal exercises or adding weight, but exercise variety and healthy eating are essential to reducing belly fat.

18. D: A PE teacher can use data that measure student learning to show students are learning, which in turn shows he or she is teaching (A); to show what students need to practice AND what they already know (B); to show which students need more help AND which students are making progress (C); and to show the value of the PE program to stakeholders (D), which can prevent or minimize PE program budget cuts, defunding, or elimination, as well as even promote PE program and funding expansion.

19. A: The self-determination theory is a psychological approach used to teach physical education to increase intrinsic student motivation by providing students with achievable but challenging tasks. Intrinsic motivation has shown most effective in fostering appreciation and lifelong physical activity engagement. Behaviorism focuses on the psychomotor domain and is a teacher-directed approach that works to change students' behaviors based on the environment the teacher creates. Social theory relies heavily on the affective domain, or the social aspects of student engagement, and underpins cooperative and sport education models where students work together to solve problems. Constructivism theory focuses on the cognitive domain and works toward providing students with an understanding of what they are doing and why in the psychomotor and affective domains.

20. D: Carlos should ensure that he has an energy balance, with the same energy coming in and going out. If the energy consumed via food is greater than his energy output through physical activity and exercise, Carlos will gain weight. If his energy intake is less than his energy output, Carlos will lose weight. If the energy input and output are not equal, Carlos may lose or gain weight depending on where the imbalance occurs.

21. A: A muscular endurance goal requires that the muscle work for longer periods of time. Therefore, the higher the rep count, the greater the endurance. Increased soreness likely indicates that the overload principle was employed without progression to meet strength goals. Maintaining the same rep count over time does not indicate improvement effectiveness but simply maintenance. Maintenance is good for individuals who have met their fitness goals, but variation in activities ensures that the body continues to respond to exercise's physiological benefits. Increasing weight over time will gradually occur with endurance, whereas increasing weight complements a strength-building increase.

22. A: The Society for Health and Physical Educators (SHAPE) America sets the national K-12 and physical education teacher education standards and each state-level SHAPE equivalent adopts these standards. Council for the Accreditation of Educator Preparation (CAEP) is responsible for accreditation of physical education teacher education programs and working closely with SHAPE America that also sets the health and physical education standards for teacher education programs. HPE is the acronym for health and physical education used in some programs. The Every Student Succeeds Act (ESSA) is a law designed to ensure equal opportunities for all students, including health and physical education.

23. C: In dual and individual sports, the expectation is that noise is minimal during gameplay. In contrast, during team sports, especially invasion games, loud noise is expected and promoted as fans cheer on their teams. In individual sports, there are only personal fouls and in team sports there are personal and team fouls, but these are rule differences rather than etiquette issues. In tennis, coaches cannot coach players during match play, but coaches can coach the entire game during team sports. These are also rules and not matters of etiquette.

24. C: Reaction time is a perceptual motor ability as it uses the senses and is dependent on the environment, such as a starting gun in track or having to play defense. Muscular strength is reliant on physiological factors and is less dependent on the environment, such as a student's coordination or ability to do push-ups.

25. B: Elementary is the most appropriate school level to teach movement education as it is the foundation for the fundamental movements (locomotor and non-locomotor), movement concepts (spatial awareness, relationships, and effort), and the three domains of learning (psychomotor, cognitive, and affective). These foundational skills and concepts aid in progressive, mature movements taught in middle and high school needed for individual and team sports, as well as fitness activities. Some pre-kindergarten programs are included in elementary school physical education programs, while others are offered at daycare centers.

26. C: Cross-training and monitoring type and amount of food intake can aid in healthy body composition. Increasing physical activity can offset some effects of consuming excessive fat. Physical activity cannot mitigate some harmful effects of excessive fat consumption, e.g., high cholesterol. Food is needed for a healthy body and should not be avoided but should be consumed in moderation. Reading food labels aids in making informed choices about foods, but reading the labels will not establish a healthy body composition if one is consuming high-fat, low-nutrient meals. Moving more is vague, and an explicit goal that is shown to be effective is missing, such as "to move 30 to 60 minutes per day."

27. D: Getting rest and eating a meal with carbohydrates will help students prepare for a cross country meet as both contribute to the athlete having more energy and reduced fatigue. Energy from carbohydrates is easier and faster to recruit than energy from fats. The race would be over before fat energy could be used. Rest also allows the body to recover from the muscular stress that occurs during exercise. A practice run one day prior may be disadvantageous as the body will likely experience a faster fatigue rate which can negatively affect performance. A walk-through of the course is recommended to familiarize the runners with the course.

28. A: Katherine should incorporate lateral deltoid raises to target the shoulders and shrugs to target the trapezius (the muscle group connecting the neck and shoulders) to prepare for the swim season. Deltoid raises can be performed laterally, posteriorly, and anteriorly, but lateral deltoid raises also work the trapezius muscles. Shoulder joint actions include flexion, extension, adduction, and abduction, but the shoulder joint is not capable of a curling action.

29. A: The teacher should address the concept of progressive overload, which is the gradual increase in weight. Students should start with low weight and gradually increase to prevent injury and extreme soreness. In circuit training, various exercises are specific to the muscle group or health-related fitness component but are general for group circuits. Specificity is not a safety measure. Regression is the principle of "if you don't use it, you lose it," or you regress or lose the gains made from training if you stop engaging in fitness activities. Spotting is a safety measure but not done during circuit training typically as the pace of activities is too fast and designed to get through several exercises quickly. Spotting is ideal for muscular strength activities that require lifting heavy amounts like squats or bench presses performed at a slower pace.

30. B: Cultural and folk dances aid in developing respect for diversity as every student's culture can be included or represented through dance. In addition to the dance steps, students are introduced to the meaning behind dances, and historical and cultural facts that pertain to each culture. There are also dances in pop culture that are associated with certain cultural groups such as contemporary line dances. Locomotor movements are activities that children across diverse groups engage or participate in, but these do not inherently foster respect for cultural diversity. Not all students can dance due to mobile disabilities, but respect for other cultures can be gained by learning about others. Non-locomotor movements are inclusive activities that are utilized in dance but do not foster respect for diversity.

31. A: Intrinsic feedback is when the performer can feel the movement internally and determine if the movement was accurate and should be repeated, like striking the ball in the center, or if a change needs to occur to improve the movement, e.g., correcting the foot striking the ball on the side rather than the center. Advanced performers use intrinsic feedback. Knowledge of results is extrinsic, or external, feedback that is evident based on the outcome, such as whether the ball went in the basket.

32. C: Hypertrophy or an increase in muscle size is an unrealistic goal for most high school students as hypertrophy usually does not occur until ages 19-22, which is hormone-related rather than training-related. Justice should be informed that he will get stronger in time and train the muscle group at least two days a week. Justice would need to wait until puberty is over for muscle size to increase. Refraining from cardiovascular activities while weight training is a myth as a healthy heart is important for well-being; however, the cardio amount may be lower than someone with a cardiovascular or weight-loss goal. Cross-training is not ideal given Justice's goal to increase muscle size as he should focus on weight lifting.

33. B: Among cooperative learning components, social skills (a) are incorporated such that students can identify their purposes and applications. Group processing (b) entails student reflection on how well the group or team functioned to work toward its learning goals. Individual accountability (c) involves all individual student members taking responsibility for group or team success, hence being accountable for it. Positive interdependence (d) entails student group work or teamwork in assigned member roles to attain shared goals.

34. B: Discipline is important when engaging in recreational activities since there is no one to monitor activity, hold the individual accountable, or help maintain motivation as would occur under the direction of a teacher or coach. The rules for recreational activities should be researched before engagement. Goals vary among individuals, but this does not explain why discipline is important. Outcome goals, such as fun, fitness, and competition tend to be clear, and creating goals helps with motivation and discipline.

35. B: Having students analyze angles of underhand and overhand throws is an example of integrated physical education or cross-curriculum approaches, as the angles of release are a physics concept but taught in a physical education environment. Commonly, schools adopt school-wide initiatives to include cross-curriculum activities to garner a deeper understanding of content. Another teacher teaching non-physical education content is cross-curricular instruction but not integrated within the physical education context. Specialists provide expert training in physical education activities. Student choice does not guarantee integration, and choices tend to be from PE curricula.

36. A: To prove a PE teacher was negligent, as to prove negligence by anyone, a plaintiff (e.g., a student or student's parents) must prove ALL four of these elements: (1) the defendant (a PE teacher in this example) had a duty to adhere to a specific standard of conduct (a); (2) the defendant breached that duty (b); (3) the defendant's breach of duty was BOTH the actual AND proximate (foreseeable) cause of injury (c); and (4) the breach caused damages to the plaintiff (d).

37. A: The skeletal muscles in the body produce voluntary movement. The smooth muscles (b) are used by the blood vessels and organs like the heart, bladder, etc., to produce involuntary movement. Therefore, both (c) and (d) are incorrect.

38. D: This physical program meets proposed guidelines in student engagement and the large teaching area. SHAPE America recommends that students are engaged in activity at least 50% of the time. The equipment ratio and class size are ineffective characteristics of a physical education program. Class size recommendations are between 25 and 35 students with a 2:1 student-to-equipment ratio.

39. D: Coach Wheelock is demonstrating low expectations and gender stereotypes of female students despite their role as basketball athletes. He assumes that they would not be able to play with the boys. He also assumes that all boys play rough, which is another gender stereotype. Rules should be in place to ensure safety for all students. As long as the girls can play basketball in class, separating groups by gender would not be considered gender discrimination or favoritism towards the boys.

40. D: Animal walks are recommended to teach these movement concepts as students can draw on prior knowledge of how animals move. Using animals allows students to identify different concepts, such as "moving like a flock of birds," to understand spatial awareness, effort, and relationships. Although stationary movements and balancing can teach some movement concepts, the lack of variety limits what can be taught. Fitness activities can teach some movement concepts, but fitness concepts are more abstract and will likely confuse younger children.

41. D: Physical education (PE) teachers must always conduct regular safety inspections of facilities and equipment on a consistent basis. Rather than using extrinsic motivations (A) like external punishments or rewards, PE teachers are advised to enhance intrinsic student motivations to be responsible for learning. When student behaviors are inappropriate, PE teachers should not ignore them (B) but address them immediately. PE teachers do need to obtain and regularly renew certification in cardiopulmonary resuscitation (CPR) and automated external defibrillator (AED) use (C).

42. B: Childhood obesity has been instrumental in the shift from team sports to health-related fitness in physical education programs. Childhood obesity is attributed to sedentary lifestyles and low-quality, high-fat foods. Technology (e.g., heart rate monitors, pedometers, activity trackers, fitness and nutrition apps) is a trend that has enhanced the tracking and measurement of health-related fitness outcomes. Health-related fitness activities help prepare students for life-long activities that are conducted during adulthood, which is an unchanged goal of the education process. Health promotion is the current focus as a result of childhood obesity and physical inactivity.

43. B: Adequate opportunities to respond (OTR) or practicing skills regularly aid in skill refinement. Tag games keep students physically active and help teach movement concepts including speed, dodging, fleeing, and chasing. Leading and following are strategies that aid in the refinement of locomotor skills. Choice is a strategy used to foster motivation to participate.

44. A: A recent trend emerging among policymakers and educators is the positive youth development perspective. This philosophy regards children and teens NOT as problems adults must manage (B) but resources for developing new or improved competencies (A). The US Department of Health and Human Services (HHS, 2008) published *Physical Activity Guidelines for Americans,* its cover stating the message, "Be active, healthy, and happy!" (C). The President's Council on Physical Fitness and Sports (2009) recommended that parents and healthcare providers, as well as educators, optimize youth development through PA (D).

45. C: Students engage in walking, jogging, and running when engaged in orienteering. In a triathlon, fitness activities include swimming, cycling, and running or jogging. Hiking, swimming, and cycling benefit muscular and cardiovascular fitness but are not skills used in orienteering.

46. A: Some students and others may be pleasantly surprised to learn that overweight and obese individuals can lower their risk of related diseases by losing only 5-10 percent of their existing body weight. In addition, overweight (not obese) individuals whose waist measurements are not disproportionately large and who have one or no other risk factors may need only maintain rather than reduce their weight.

47. C: Tests on which students must write answers are least useful for assessing their performance of physical education skills, which typically must be physically demonstrated. Observational checklists are more useful as teachers can watch students perform the skills to be assessed and mark whether they can do them or not or mark the degree to which they have mastered them. Rating scales of skill level are more useful as teachers can observe student skill performance and then rate the level of mastery or skill they have attained on a scale with degrees between most and least. Graphs of performance data are more useful as teachers can record numbers of successful demonstrations per session as points and connect these to form a line or curve showing progress over time. Graphs also can include a line indicating a criterion for reference, so performance points can be seen above, below, and at this line.

48. A: Michael should stop working out and go to the nurse to make sure there is no medical issue. Allowing him to continue exercising may pose harm. A talk test is another tool used to determine intensity, but the heart rate monitor is more accurate and supersedes the talk test. While blood pressure and heart rate are health indicators, they do not increase at the same rates. A low heart rate is not an indicator of hypertension; therefore, taking his blood pressure would be meaningless.

49. D: The chronic bacterial outbreaks are likely attributed to failing to take a shower after physical education class. Cleaning the body after moderate to vigorous physical activity reduces bacteria growth thus lowering the risk of disease. Coughing is usually associated with a cold, which is a viral infection. Most conditions that result from skin-to-skin contact or rolling around on mats are viral or fungal. Ringworm is a common example.

50. A: Exercise depletes the muscles' glycogen stores, so within the first 30 minutes to two hours after exercising, participants should eat or drink simple carbohydrates while muscles absorb them better. Students and others with inadequate diets may need vitamin-mineral supplements, but with balanced nutrition, these are generally unnecessary (b). Although adequate daily hydration is critical in both everyday activities and exercise, it is a myth that everybody needs eight glasses a day (c): amount of fluid loss determines amount of water needed. Vitamins do not supply energy (d); they help release chemical energy from foods.

51. B: Some basic body positions to teach in PE include the sit (a), pike (b), tuck (c), straddle (d) sit, straddle stand, T-stand; front, side, and rear support; and tuck to front support, front support to tuck, front support to straddle stand, straddle stand to front support, and front support to rear support. Of these, the pike (b) position is one which many movement stunts often pass through, begin with, or end with, so PE teachers should give students demonstrations, instructions, and practice in it.

52. B: Back extensions will help with posture by increasing flexibility in the lower back, which causes the shoulders to pull back to an upright position. Kyphosis is an age-related hunched back condition that generally occurs in older women and differs from the hunched back postures among some students. Curl-ups may further the rounded or hunched back posture. A counter-balance exercise including push-ups would aid in posture corrections. The pec deck may also aid in the rounding of shoulders and back. A counter-balance exercise including rear delts would help with posture.

53. A: A chasse is a ballet step adopted in jazz and modern dance and is similar to the gallop where one foot leads and the other follows. An axel is a turn used in jazz and modern dance but consists of turning while hopping. The ball change is a transition step used in jazz that consists of transferring weight on the balls of the feet, similar to the weight transfer that occurs in the grapevine step. The drop is an intentional fall to the ground, often after performing a leap.

54. A: The teacher is responsible for informing students of the safety rules and posting the rules around the gym. The teacher can provide links to school-wide information as a courtesy, but the school leadership team is responsible for disseminating safety plans to parents and students. School leadership personnel are also required to have emergency exit and fire drill protocols posted. The teacher is responsible for implementing fire drill expectations.

55. C: The teacher needs to teach or re-teach the difference between body size and fitness and address the myth that someone who is thin is more fit than someone who is not. An individual can be both fit and overweight or obese, although carrying extra weight disproportionate to one's body frame increases disease risks. With training, small and large individuals can gain high levels of cardiovascular fitness. Thin individuals can also have too much body fat for their stature, referred to as "skinny fat," and can have low fitness levels. These skinny fat individuals are also at increased disease risks. The adage, "you cannot judge a book by its cover," can be applied here, as fitness cannot be determined by merely looking at a person's shape.

56. B: Students in grades K-2 should be able to demonstrate progress toward more complexity in manipulative motor skills (C). Students in grades 3-5 should be able to refine and apply complex manipulative skills in the context of lead-up games (A). Students in grades 6-8 should be able to apply basic and advanced manipulative skills to sports, dance, and gymnastics, individually and on teams (D). Students in grades 9-12 should be able to create their own advanced movement skills and use them (B).

57. B: An equipment-specific adaptation or modification would be helpful and might consist of using bright colors which should be easier for the student with vision impairment to see. The task remains the same, but the object or equipment is adjusted or modified to meet the student's needs. A task-specific adaptation would change the task itself by moving the student closer to the target; however, the student can shoot the arrow; therefore, the task would not change. The boundaries would remain the same as the student's only issue is seeing the colors on the archery targets.

58. D: "The student will skip using a mature pattern" is an example of a SHAPE America grade level outcome for students in grade 1, as it is explicit about what students are expected to do, while "the student will demonstrate motor skills" is a SHAPE America standard that is broad or general. Students will also apply movement concepts and it is hoped that students recognize value in physical activity, but these too are general standards rather than explicit outcomes.

59. D: Circuit training is an effective method to teach all of the health-related activities when there is limited time, as dedication to each component can be included. Resistance training can be included in circuit training, but performed independently, it addresses only muscular strength and muscular endurance—two health-related fitness components. Interval training is inherent in circuit training as there is a particular time or amount of activity followed by transitional rest periods. Intervals can also be explicit within circuit training but do not guarantee coverage of all health-related fitness components independently and are often used for cardiovascular fitness. Fartlek training is speed training for running and does not provide well-rounded coverage of the health-related fitness components.

60. C: Levels of responsibility defining positive youth development goals incorporate self-management skills, including **self-control**, exemplified by respecting others' feeling and rights (a) and approaching conflict resolution democratically (d); **self-motivation**, shown in trying out new tasks and persistence on tasks (b) and exemplifying effort; and **self-direction**, exemplified by working independently, setting goals progressively (c), and resisting peer pressure.

61. B: For exercise to be aerobic, it must involve continuous movement, not stop-and-start movement, to elevate the heart and respiratory rates for sustained durations. Aerobic exercise uses the large muscle groups, not small (a). It typically does NOT firm or tone muscles (c) due to low resistance; weight training does. Another common misconception is that aerobic exercise must be of low intensity to burn fat (d); research finds sufficient exercise at any intensity can reduce fat.

62. D: Generally, students learn PE skills better by viewing and imitating demonstrations (A) than hearing explanations or descriptions, but demonstration by itself works best for students with mainly visual learning styles. Students with logical, mathematical, or visual learning styles benefit from adding diagrams to demonstrations (B). Students with kinesthetic learning styles benefit from being physically guided through skill movements in addition to seeing them demonstrated (C). Students with verbal learning styles benefit from adding spoken explanations or descriptions to demonstrations (D).

63. A: Companies like Biokinetics (www.biokinetics.com) use different machinery, software, and procedures to test sports equipment like helmets against official standards. While drop tests from towers traditionally test helmet impact performance, this method cannot accurately test football head-to-head collision impacts (b) because players collide at much higher speeds; linear impact tests, with rams hitting auto crash-simulation headforms, are used (a). Different tests and apparatus test helmet retention system stretch rather than strength and stability (c). Helmet mouthguards not only protect teeth, but also brains from concussions (d); headforms with articulating mandibles test this.

64. A: To attain the fastest acceleration, a sprinter should keep the center of gravity as high as possible while crouching in the starting block. As the sprinter accelerates, the upper body rises with forward body propulsion. Having the center of gravity lowest (b), between high and low (c), or starting in the full upright body position (d) will allow less speed in accelerating.

65. B: Integrated physical education is a cross-curricular approach where two or more areas of study are taught together. In this example, students may not only learn how to perform the overhand throw (biomechanics), but may also learn about the angle of release, projectile motion, and force (Physics). Exercise and sport science are sub-disciplines of kinesiology that study human movement in exercise and sport settings. Physical education is also a sub-discipline of kinesiology that studies human movement in schools or pedagogy.

66. D: The teacher should take attendance before and after the hike to ensure that all students are present, as people can get lost on hiking trails. Applying sunscreen and having a charged cell phone are important safety factors. School leadership and the physical education team should be given advance notice that students are being taken out for a hike. Student-leaders can be helpful but are not a procedural practice.

67. B: The change in heart rate is likely a decrease in fitness. An increase in heart rate may indicate a respiratory condition or infection, but the normal resting heart rate range is 60 to 100 bpm. Hence, a resting heart rate of 83 bpm is within normal limits. A consistent resting heart rate above 100 bpm is likely tachycardia, or fast heart rate. It could indicate illness or a life-threatening condition. In this case, the teacher should inform the student, notify a parent or guardian, and school nurse if available. A fast heart rate is not likely an indicator of heart disease. High blood pressure and obesity are risk indicators of heart disease.

68. B: Proprioceptive neuromuscular facilitation (PNF) has been shown to have the most significant improvements for flexibility. It consists of variations of the four types of stretches with a contraction-relaxation pattern. Active stretching is typically an unassisted static stretch where the individual provides the force of the stretch, e.g., quad stretch. Passive stretching is an assisted stretch where someone or an object aids in deepening the stretch. Both active and passive stretching can be static or dynamic. Dynamic stretches are performed with movement and preferred for warm-ups for secondary-aged students. Ballistic stretches are bouncy or jerky and should be avoided to reduce the risk of overstretching or other injury.

69. B: Jacquan needs to create an energy imbalance where he burns more fuel or calories than food or calorie consumption. Energy balance (C), or homeostasis (A), is equal amounts of energy in and energy out and is ideal for individuals who want to maintain their current weight. Energy drinks (D) often contain excessive amounts of sugar and caffeine. They are not generally recommended to include in a weight loss program, as too much sugar can impede weight-loss goals.

70. C: Negligence has occurred as the teacher did not ensure a safe environment by cleaning the spill. While not intentional, the teacher may be held liable. Accountability (A) is holding the teacher to certain standards. There may be a consequence for the incident. The circumstance may also be considered an accident where the teacher can be given a reminder to check the floors throughout instruction, especially after water breaks. Misfeasance (B) is a type of negligence that occurs when a teacher incorrectly implements a policy or practice. Malfeasance (D) is an act where the teacher intentionally breaks the law.

71. D: Moving creatively to varied music rhythms using simple dance steps (A) is a movement skill competency suitable for students in the first grade. Jumping rope to the tempo of music, both singly and with a partner (B), is suitable for students in the second grade. Bouncing, passing, and catching a ball to match a musical rhythm (C) is suitable for students in the third grade. Expressing feelings or ideas through rhythmic motion, with and without music (D), is suitable for students in the fifth grade.

72. D: FITT = Frequency, Intensity, Time, Type. Overload increases fitness by increasing workload so the body adapts and can do more. Increasing number of workout days increases Frequency for BOTH resistance AND cardio training. Different exercise (A) changes Type for cardio training; for resistance training, this would involve different exercises BUT the same body area. Increasing repetitions (B) increases Time for resistance training; for cardio, one would increase duration. Increasing resistance (C) increases Intensity for weight training; for cardio, one would increase pace or percentage of maximum heartrate.

73. C: Catching is a manipulative skill that is classified as receptive, i.e., the catcher *receives* a moving ball or other object that another player has thrown, kicked, or stricken. Kicking (a), striking (b), and throwing (d) are all manipulative skills classified as propulsive, i.e., a player *propels* the ball or other object to make it move through the air, across a surface, etc.

74. A: The air bicycle, done lying on the back, hands behind head, legs elevated, making bicycle-pedaling movements in the air while crunching by alternately touching each elbow to the opposite knee, strengthens the abdominal muscles. The alien squat (b) targets the quadriceps (front thigh) muscles. The axle deadlift (c), using barbells, targets the lower-back muscles. The dumbbell curl (d) strengthens the biceps (inner upper arm) muscles.

75. A: The teacher is demonstrating a type of formative assessment, which is used to identify student strengths and weaknesses, and provide feedback on how to improve or refine. Formative assessment is also called assessment *of* learning, whereas assessment *for* learning is summative assessment, which identifies what students have learned and comes at the end of the unit or lesson. Assessment *as* learning are self-assessments that students engage in to monitor their own progress and make changes accordingly, which aid in deepening understanding of the tasks.

76. C: Bandura identified and described observational learning. Among factors influencing it, he included Attention (a), meaning students must observe the teacher or model; Retention (b), meaning students must encode and store movement patterns in memory for retrieval; Motor Reproduction (c), meaning students repeatedly practice the kinesthetic and neuromuscular patterns modeled until they can imitate them; and Incentives and Reinforcement (d), which motivate students to perform the others.

77. C: Free weight exercises help improve flexibility and posture. These exercises are conducted using a full range of motion at the joints and strengthening muscles that aid in keeping the body in an upright position. Isometric exercises are those that use static positions that require muscular resistance, such as wall sits and planks, and do not allow for a repeated range of motion. Running reduces flexibility as the repetitive motion strengthens but tightens the muscles.

78. D: Beginning students make lots of errors and focus heavily on skill cues, so the teacher needs to be intentional and direct with instruction to help the student understand the movements of the skill. As students begin to understand the movement as illustrated in improvement, the need for direct feedback and demonstrations are reduced.

79. A: Kimberly needs to hear or see the skill cue to "step with the opposite foot of your throwing arm" to remind her of the movements. Practice will only work if Kimberly is practicing the correct movements. Working with a partner may or may not work, as it depends on the skill level of the partner. While all students may not master every skill, cues to help students improve should continue.

80. A: Although student health risks are generally shared with physical education teachers from school personnel, administering a Physical Activity Readiness Questionnaire (PAR-Q) is a simple proactive measure to identify potential health risks associated with cardiovascular and endurance training. A PAR-Q asks students/participants/parents to respond to health history questions that may negatively impact activity such as a history of asthma or musculoskeletal injuries. Athletics and sports programs require physicals for participation, but they are generally not required in physical education programs. A proper warm-up reduces the risk of injury as it prepares the body for vigorous activity when engaging in cardiovascular activities. However, a warm-up does not identify potential health risks. A talk test is a self-evaluation of exercise intensity.

81. A: Student choice has been shown to increase student motivation as it empowers students to make their own decisions rather than the teacher directing instruction. Physical education models of choice include cooperative learning, adventure education, sport education, and Teaching Games for Understanding (TGfU). Direct instruction and traditional teaching approaches are teacher-driven and based on the teacher's decisions. Competitive instruction has been shown to motivate highly athletic students but de-motivate less athletic or competitive students.

82. C: Rhythmic activities like dance and creative movements help students learn to control their bodies. While music is often used, the primary goal is body control. Locomotor, non-locomotor, and manipulative movements are used during rhythmic activities which can aid in the performance of skills, like gymnastics or dance routines.

83. A: Title IX gives women and girls equal access to sport and education. Roe v. Wade is the Supreme Court case that gave women the legal right to an abortion, subsequently overturned in 2022. The Civil Rights Act is a law that prohibits discrimination based on race, color, religion, or country of origin in schools, employment, and public spaces. The Women's Rights Act is a civil rights act that protects women from discrimination based on gender, which was not included in the Civil Rights Act.

84. C: Planks are body weight training exercises that strengthen the muscles in the torso. Squats (a), lunges (b), and bridges (d) are all body weight training exercises that strengthen muscles in the legs and buttocks.

85. D: To improve muscular endurance, one should engage in lifting low weight at high repetitions (reps) as the goal is to prepare the muscles to work for long periods of time e.g., running marathons and holding planks and squats. To improve muscular strength, one should engage in high weight and low reps to allow for muscle hypertrophy. When training for muscular endurance, muscular strength improves but at a slower rate. When training for muscular strength, muscular endurance also improves but more slowly, as the training is specific to the muscular strength goal.

86. A: Recovery heart rate should be taken by feeling the pulse for 15 seconds after cooling down, 5-6 minutes after the last aerobic exercise. It should not be taken before cooling down (b), during cooldown (c), or in between exercises (d). Recovery heart rate should be 120 beats per minute (bpm) or lower for safeness and effectiveness, if higher, the next workouts' intensity should be lowered.

87. D: Balance provides stability and control needed for movement tasks. Agility can be defined various ways, but it usually refers to a combination of speed, effort, and ability to change positions and directions quickly. Balance is necessary for all motor skills, but it plays a particularly large role in changing directions in agility-based tasks. One example of use of balance in an agility-based tasks is running cone-drills with fast changes in direction. These types of tasks are impossible to perform well in if the athlete is not in control of their balance.

88. A: The numerous benefits of physical activity engagement are why physical activity is promoted in physical education programs. Consistent physical activity engagement reduces the risk of heart disease and other health conditions and improves mental health outcomes. Physical activity reduces blood pressure. Sedentary activities and poor dietary intake increase blood pressure risks. Engaging in muscular fitness activities lead to muscle hypertrophy and prevents atrophy or the wasting of muscle. Endorphins or "happy hormones" are released during physical activity which is another benefit of physical activity.

89. D: At Level 0, irresponsibility (B), students may "put down" classmates, verbally intimidate them, interrupt others, and are unmotivated. At Level 1, self-control (A), students control themselves enough not to interfere with classmate participation and learning, but they may not fully participate themselves. At Level 2, involvement (C), students are involved actively in learning and open to trying new activities. At Level 3, self-responsibility, students more responsible for their actions can work unsupervised. At Level 4, caring (D), students extend responsibility through cooperation, concern, support, and help with or for classmates.

90. A: Typically, schools require students and their parents or guardians to sign the Agreement to Participate form, to acknowledge student and parent awareness of the inherent risks of participating in PE activities, and to confirm student agreement to participate and comply with safety regulations for all activities. K-12 schools do not limit signatories to only parents (B) or only students (C), and do not require PE teachers to sign (D).

Constructed Response

91. This is the rubric used to score constructed-response questions on the CSET.

Purpose	The extent to which the response addresses the constructed-response assignment's charge in relation to relevant CSET content specifications or subject matter requirements.
Subject Matter Knowledge	Application of accurate subject matter knowledge as described in the relevant CSET content specifications or subject matter requirements.
Support	The appropriateness and quality of the supporting evidence in relation to relevant CSET content specifications or subject matter requirements.

Score Point	Score Point Description
3	**The "3" response reflects command of the relevant knowledge and skills as defined in the CSET content specifications or subject matter requirements.** • The purpose of the assignment is fully achieved. • There is an accurate application of relevant content specifications or subject matter requirements. • There is appropriate and specific relevant supporting evidence.
2	**The "2" response reflects general command of the relevant knowledge and skills as defined in the CSET content specifications or subject matter requirements.** • The purpose of the assignment is largely achieved. • There is a largely accurate application of relevant content specifications or subject matter requirements. • There is acceptable relevant supporting evidence.
1	**The "1" response reflects limited or no command of the relevant knowledge and skills as defined in the CSET content specifications or subject matter requirements.** • The purpose of the assignment is only partially or not achieved. • There is limited or no application of relevant content specifications or subject matter requirements. • There is little or no relevant supporting evidence.
U	**The "U" (unscorable) is assigned to a response that is unrelated to the assignment, illegible, primarily in a language other than English, or does not contain a sufficient amount of original work to score.**
B	**The "B" (blank) is assigned to a response that is blank.**